GREAT PAINTINGS

from the

NATIONAL GALLERY OF ART

Edited by

HUNTINGTON CAIRNS

and

JOHN WALKER

THE MACMILLAN COMPANY: NEW YORK

U. S. NATIONAL GALLERY OF ART

SMITHSONIAN INSTITUTION, WASHINGTON, D. C.

1952

FOREWORD

By David E. Finley

Director, National Gallery of Art

This book is a companion volume to the one published by the National Gallery of Art in 1944. In each case an attempt has been made, by means of color reproductions as faithful as mechanical means permit, to present some of the great paintings now housed in the National Gallery in Washington.

The two volumes contain reproductions of only a portion of the works of art that comprise the Gallery's collection. They do, however, give some idea of the wealth of painting that has come to the National Gallery during the eleven years it has been in existence. And the reproductions and accompanying texts will have served their purpose if they evoke in people in this country and throughout the world a desire to come to Washington and see the works of art available here.

To arouse such a desire is not difficult with the aid of color reproductions which, if faithfully executed, have that "magical power of evocation" so admired by James Huneker and so seldom possessed by even the most eloquent critics. Fortunately today the desire to see great paintings can be gratified by visits not only to Washington but to many cities in this country where museums exist with comprehensive and well arranged collections of the highest quality.

When the present century opened, there were few large museums in the United States and even fewer collections of works of art of the first importance, such as had existed for centuries in Europe. Today the situation is very different, owing to the generosity of public-spirited citizens, such as Mr. Mellon, Mr. Kress, Mr. Joseph Widener and his father, Mr. Peter A. B. Widener, Mr. Chester Dale, Mr. Lessing Rosenwald and others who have established great collections in Washington and throughout the country that rank in quality and scope with those to be found in other parts of the civilized world.

As a result of these splendid gifts and of wise purchases on the part of trustees, the American people now have the opportunity to study the progress of successive civilizations, as illustrated by the works of art assembled in our museums. This is particularly true in the field of Western painting, so that artists can find in this country, by studying the fine examples available here, the knowledge and the inspiration for which it was formerly necessary to go to Europe. Less than a hundred years ago American artists, such as Whistler, Sargent, and Mary Cassatt, felt obliged to go to France and England and Italy to study the great paintings which could be found there but not in their own country.

Today the National Gallery in Washington and other American museums are in a position to do the two things for which they were created: first, to set up and maintain a standard of quality by collecting, preserving, and exhibiting to the best advantage the finest works of art obtainable in their chosen fields; and second, to make those works of art known and enjoyed by the people of this country and, indeed, by people everywhere to whom, in the larger sense, these and all works of art belong.

The responsibility imposed on our museums is all the greater because so many of our public schools, our colleges and universities are not doing what might be expected of them in the field of art education. Many have no courses in this subject and still consider art of minor interest as compared, for instance, with science.

In recent years the trend in this country has been to emphasize technological or vocational training, with the result that men and women are becoming specialized, knowing only their own subject. On other subjects their critical faculties are becoming dulled, so that too often they accept, more or less without question, what the critics, the commentators, the writers of books, tell them. They accept it notwithstanding the fact that many of these authorities are inclined to condemn what they do not like or do not understand or consider intellectually unfashionable at the moment.

In the field of art, on the other hand, too many people are inclined to pass judgment on what is or is not excellent long before they have earned the right to do so. In other fields, in which they are not qualified, they show more reticence, but not as regards a work of art, which is too often dismissed as of no importance because it does not happen to appeal to their particular taste or because they do not understand what the artist is trying to say.

"Seeing," says Bernard Berenson, "is as much an acquired art as speaking, although no doubt easier to learn." Here the museum can be of help in arriving at an informed judgment, based on such facts and knowledge as are available. Most important of all, it can provide the opportunity to become familiar with great art, preferably as it came from the hand of the artist but, if that is not possible, as shown in color reproductions, such as the ones in this book, which prepare us to see and enjoy the original work of art when the opportunity comes to us.

For most people the acquisition of such knowledge is largely a matter of self-education, once the discipline of school and university has been removed. And in education the problem today is the same as it has always been: to define the standards by which education is to be regulated. The museum is in a position to define with some precision the standard of excellence in art. To that extent it gives a standard for education, at least in the field of the arts; and it also provides an opportunity for the average man and woman to learn something of the satisfying and enduring nature of cultural values, which neither time nor changing circumstances can take from us.

The museum and its related activities offer one of the few existing means to achieve that end. It is in furtherance of that end that the present volume has been published.

PREFACE

This volume, like its predecessor, *Masterpieces of Painting from the National Gallery of Art*, published in 1944, contains eighty-five reproductions in color from the collections of the National Gallery of Art. None of the paintings here reproduced, and none of the authors from whom we have drawn the accompanying texts, appeared in the earlier volume. The texts have been selected as often as possible, for the general discussions, with the idea of presenting a consistent attitude towards art; but in instances where the artists themselves appear to be dominated by a contrary view we have sought for corresponding texts.

The color plates were produced from separation negatives made directly from the original paintings, and the proofs were then corrected against the paintings as often as necessary to insure the highest possible degree of color fidelity. The plates were printed on two-color Miehle flat-bed cylinder presses; the yellow and red plates were run off first, the blue and black plates thereafter. Throughout the printing the presses were run at reduced speed in order to obtain a better register and as continuous a color accuracy as possible.

H. C.

J. W.

ACKNOWLEDGMENTS

The editors wish to thank members of the staff of the National Gallery of Art, especially Colonel Harry A. McBride for his contribution to the design and execution of this volume. They are also indebted to Dr. Elio Gianturco and Mr. Herman G. Weinberg for help with special translations.

The following libraries have been of assistance in making source material available: Detroit Public Library, Detroit, Mich.; Freer Gallery of Art Library, Washington, D. C.; Harvard University Library, Cambridge, Mass.; Library of Congress, Washington, D. C.; New York University Libraries, New York City; Ohio State University Library, Columbus, Ohio; Princeton University Library, Princeton, N. J.; Public Library of the District of Columbia, Washington, D. C.; University of Illinois Library, Urbana, Ill.; Yale University Library, New Haven, Conn.

For permission to reproduce copyrighted material in this work acknowledgment is made to the following publishers and others: from *The Civilization of the Renaissance in Italy*, by Jacob Burckhardt, by permission of George Allen & Unwin Ltd., London; from *The Analects of Confucius*, by permission of George Allen & Unwin Ltd., London; from *Life, Art, and Letters of George Inness*, by George Inness, Jr., by permission of Appleton-Century-Crofts, Inc., New York; from *The Psychology of Art*, Volume I, by André Malraux, published in Bollingen Series by the Bollingen Foundation, Inc., New York, and by courtesy of A. Zwemmer Ltd., London; from *Bird-Watching and Bird Behaviour*, by Julian Huxley, by permission of Chatto and Windus, London; from *Giovanni di Paolo*, by John Pope-Hennessy, by permission of Chatto and Windus, London; from *The Testament of Beauty*, by Robert Bridges, by permission of The Clarendon Press, Oxford; from *Biographia Literaria*, by S. T. Coleridge, by permission of The Clarendon Press, Oxford; from *The Poems of John Donne*, by permission of The Clarendon Press, Oxford; from *Longinus on the Sublime*, by permission of The Clarendon Press, Oxford; from "Taste," by Osbert Sitwell and Margaret Barton (*Johnson's England*, edited by A. S. Turberville, The Clarendon Press, Oxford, 1933); from *The Journal of Eugène Dela-*

croix, translated by Walter Pach, copyright, 1948, Crown Publishers, two selections used by permission of Crown Publishers, Inc., New York; reprinted by permission of Dodd, Mead & Company, New York, and Faber and Faber Ltd., London, from *The Anatomy of Art*, by Herbert Read; from *The Note-Books of Samuel Butler*, by permission of E. P. Dutton & Co., Inc., New York, and Jonathan Cape Limited, London, and the executors of Samuel Butler; from *Hans Holbein the Younger*, by Ford Madox Ford, by permission of E. P. Dutton & Co., Inc., New York, and Gerald Duckworth & Co. Ltd., London; from *A Call to Order*, by Jean Cocteau, translated by Rollo H. Myers, by permission of Jean Cocteau, and Faber and Faber Ltd., London; from *Art and Science*, by Adrian Stokes, by permission of Faber and Faber Ltd., London; from *Landmarks in Nineteenth-Century Painting*, by Clive Bell, by permission of Harcourt, Brace and Company, Inc., New York, and Chatto and Windus, London; quoted from *The Unquiet Grave*, by permission of the author, Cyril Connolly, and the publishers, Harper & Brothers, New York, and Hamish Hamilton Ltd., London; from *History of Art*, by Élie Faure, by permission of Harper & Brothers, New York; from *Ananias or the False Artist*, by Walter Pach, by permission of Harper & Brothers, New York; from *Gilbert Stuart*, by William T. Whitley, 1932, reprinted by permission of Harvard University Press, Cambridge, Mass.; from *A History of Italian Painting* and *Western European Painting of the Renaissance*, by Frank Jewett Mather, Jr., by permission of Henry Holt and Company, Inc., New York; from *The Life and Works of Winslow Homer*, by William Howe Downes, by permission of Houghton Mifflin Company, Boston; from *The Paintings of George Bellows*, by George Bellows, by permission of Alfred A. Knopf, Inc., New York; from *The Journals of André Gide*, translated by Justin O'Brien, by permission of Alfred A. Knopf, Inc., New York; from *Adventures in the Arts*, by Marsden Hartley, copyright by Boni & Liveright, Inc., 1921 and 1949, published by Liveright Publishing Corporation, New York; from "The Desirable Life," by Raymond Mortimer, in *The Arts*, 1946, by permission of Percy Lund, Humphries & Co., Ltd., London; from *Winslow Homer*, by Lloyd Goodrich, copyright 1944 by The Macmillan Company, New York, and used with their permission; from *Science and the Modern World*, by Alfred North Whitehead, copyright 1925 by The Macmillan Company, New York, and used with their permission, and by permission of the Cambridge University Press, London; from "Art and Ideas" and "Poetry and Tradition," in *Essays*, by William Butler Yeats, copyright 1924 by The Macmillan Company, New York, and used with their permission, and by permission of Mrs. W. B. Yeats; from *Sandro Botticelli*, by Yukio Yashiro, by permission of The Medici Society Ltd., London; from *Vermeer of Delft*, by E. V. Lucas, by permission of Methuen & Co. Ltd., London; from *An Essay on Landscape Painting*, by Kuo Hsi, The Wisdom of the East Series, by permission of John Murray (Publishers) Ltd., London; from *The History of Impressionism*, by John Rewald, by permission of The Museum of Modern Art, New York; from *Mysticism and Logic*, by Bertrand Russell, by permission of W. W. Norton & Company, Inc., New York, and George Allen & Unwin Ltd., London; from *Poems of Gerard Manley Hopkins*, by permission of Oxford University Press, London; from *The Essays of Montaigne*, by permission of Oxford University Press, London; from *Artists on Art*, compiled and edited by Robert Goldwater and Marco Treves, by permission of Pantheon Books, Inc., New York; from *Religious Art from the Twelfth to the Eighteenth Century*, by Émile Mâle, by permission of Pantheon Books, Inc., New York, and Routledge and Kegan Paul Ltd., London; from *Camille Pissarro: Letters to His Son Lucien*, edited, with the assistance of Lucien Pissarro, by John Rewald, by permission of Pantheon Books, Inc., New York; from *The Georgics of Virgil*, translated by C. Day Lewis, by permission of A. D. Peters Ltd., London, and Jonathan Cape Limited, London; from *The Leadership of Giorgione*, by Duncan Phillips, by permission of the author; from *The Gentle Art of Making Enemies*, by James A. McNeill Whistler, by permission of G. P. Putnam's Sons, New York, and William Heinemann, Ltd., London; from *The Autobiography of William Carlos Williams*, copyright, 1951, by William Carlos Williams, reprinted by courtesy of Random House, Inc., New York; from *Speculations*, by T. E. Hulme, by permission of Routledge and Kegan Paul Ltd., London; from *Landscape into Art*, by Kenneth Clark, by permission of Charles Scribner's Sons, New York, and John Murray (Publishers) Ltd., London; reprinted from *Poems: 1922–1947*, by Allen Tate, copyright 1932, 1937, 1948 by Charles Scribner's Sons, New York, used by permission of the publishers, and by permission of Eyre & Spottiswoode (Publishers) Limited, London; from *Goya*, by William Rothenstein, by permission of The Unicorn Press Ltd., London; from *A Portrait of the Artist as a Young Man*, by James Joyce, by permission of The Viking Press, Inc., New York, and Jonathan Cape Limited, London.

For some selections the editors have made use of translations already available, as follows: Alberti, *The Painting of Leon Battista Alberti*, translated by Giacomo Leoni; Anonymous, *Pervigilium Veneris*, translated by Allen Tate *(Poems: 1922–1947)*; Aristotle, *Poetics*, translated by W. Hamilton Fyfe; Athanasius, *The Life of Saint Anthony*, translated by E. A. Wallis Budge *(The Book of Paradise)*; Balzac, *The Unknown Masterpiece*, translated by Ellen Marriage; Burckhardt, *The Civilization of the Renaissance in Italy*, translated by S. G. C. Middlemore; Cocteau, *A Call to Order*, translated by Rollo H. Myers; *The Analects of Confucius*, translated by Arthur Waley; *The Journal of Eugène Delacroix*, translated by Walter Pach; *Conversations of Goethe with Eckermann*, translated by John Oxenford; Faure, *History of Art*, translated by Walter Pach; *The Journals of André Gide*, translated by Justin O'Brien; Grimm, *Correspondence*, anonymous translation; Kuo Hsi, *An Essay on Landscape Painting*, translated by Shio Sakanishi; Lessing, *Laokoon*, anonymous revision of E. C. Beasley's translation; *Longinus on the Sublime*, translated by A. O. Prickard; Mâle, *Religious Art from the Twelfth to the Eighteenth Century*, anonymous translation; Malraux, *The Psychology of Art*, translated by Stuart Gilbert; *The Essays of Montaigne*, translated by E. J. Trechmann; *Camille Pissarro: Letters to His Son Lucien*, translated by Lionel Abel; Plutarch, *Moralia*, translated by Frank Cole Babbitt; Poussin, in *Artists on Art*, translated by Marco Treves; Schopenhauer, *The World as Will and Idea*, translated by R. B. Haldane and J. Kemp, with revisions by the editors; *The Aeneid of Virgil*, translated by John Dryden; *The Georgics of Virgil*, translated by C. Day Lewis.

We also wish to credit the following sources: Anonymous (fifteenth century), from *Early English Lyrics*, chosen by E. K. Chambers and F. Sidgwick, 1907; Paul Cézanne, from *Nouvelles Théories*, by Maurice Denis, 1922.

CONTENTS

9

GREAT PAINTINGS

FROM THE

NATIONAL GALLERY OF ART

MASOLINO · Florentine 1384-c. 1435

The Annunciation

As I lay up on a night
My thought was on a berd so bright
That men clepen Marye full of might,
    Redemptoris mater.

To here cam Gabriel with light,
And seid 'Heil be thou, blissful wight,
To ben clepèd now art thou dight
    Redemptoris mater.'

At that wurd that lady bright
Anon conseived God full of might.
Than men wist weel that sche hight
    Redemptoris mater.

Whan Jhesu on the rode was pight,
Mary was doolful of that sight,
Til sche sey him rise up right,
    Redemptoris mater.

Jhesu, that sittest in hevenè light,
Graunt us to comen beforn thy sight,
With that berd that is so bright,
    Redemptoris mater.

Anonymous (15th Century)

Poetry and picture are arts of a like nature, and both are busy about imitation. It was excellently said of Plutarch, poetry was a speaking picture, and picture a mute poesy. For they both invent, feign, and devise many things, and accommodate all they invent to the use and service of Nature. Yet of the two the pen is more noble than the pencil; for that can speak to the understanding, the other but to the sense. They both behold pleasure and profit as their common object; but should abstain from all base pleasures, lest they should err from their end, and, while they seek to better men's minds, destroy their manners. They both are born artificers, not made. Nature is more powerful in them than study.

Ben Jonson
Timber: or, Discoveries (1640)

Glossary: *berd*, maiden; *pight*, fastened.

The elaborate architecture and the rich patterns and sinuous folds of drapery in this panel are characteristic of a way of painting found throughout Europe toward the end of the fourteenth and the beginning of the fifteenth century. But Masolino, though himself conservative and familiar with this international style as practiced not only in Italy but also in Hungary where he traveled, formed a partnership with one of the greatest innovators in art, Masaccio. From this association with a young and brilliant genius, Masolino must have received certain progressive ideas, especially regarding the linear representation of perspective. Longhi (*Critica d'Arte*, 1940) has suggested that this painting was originally in the Church of San Niccolò Oltrarno, and therefore was the picture which Vasari saw in that church a hundred years later and praised for its accurate perspective rendering. Collections: The Earls of Wemyss, Gosford House, Longniddry, Scotland; Goldman, New York. *Mellon Collection*, 1937. Wood. Height 58¼ in.; width 45¼ in. (1.48 x 1.15). Painted c. 1430.

DOMENICO VENEZIANO · Florentine c. 1400-1461

Madonna and Child

A word as to colour. One can only give warnings against possible faults; it is clearly impossible to teach colour by words, even ever so little of it, though it can be taught in a workshop, at least partially. Well, I should say, be rather restrained than over-luxurious in colour, or you weary the eye. Do not attempt over-refinements in colour, but be frank and simple. If you look at the pieces of colouring that most delight you in ornamental work, as, e.g., a Persian carpet, or an illuminated book of the Middle Ages, and analyse its elements, you will, if you are not used to the work, be surprised at the simplicity of it, the few tints used, the modesty of the tints, and therewithal the clearness and precision of all boundary lines. In all fine flat colouring, there are regular systems of dividing colour from colour. Above all, don't attempt iridescent blendings of colour which look like decomposition. They are about as much as possible the reverse of useful.

WILLIAM MORRIS
Address (Feb. 21, 1894)

Among Florentine artists influenced by Fra Angelico was the mysterious and rare painter Domenico Veneziano. Little is known of his life and barely a dozen of his paintings have survived. According to Vasari, Domenico was invited from Venice to Florence "on account of the new method he had acquired of painting in oil." His technique, however, now seems less unusual than his choice of color. He was fond of piquant contrasts of rose and green, of tonal dissonances new in painting. He typifies that constant search after novelty which marked Florentine art in the fifteenth century. The discoveries of his generation are also suggested by such details as the correct foreshortening of the halos and the flowers, and by the improved anatomical drawing of the Christ Child. The rose hedge in the background may be a reference to the Virgin as the mystic rose of the litany, or to her identification with the Old Testament Bride who sang in the Song of Solomon: "I am the rose of Sharon." Heavenly love is symbolized by the red roses and purity by the white. Purity is further stressed by the omission of thorns from the rose hedge, for, according to Saint Ambrose, the rose had grown in heaven without thorns and had acquired them only after the fall of man, to remind man of his sins. The Virgin is therefore sometimes described as the "rose without thorns." Collections: Edgeworth family, Edgeworthstown, Ireland. *Samuel H. Kress Collection*, 1939. Wood. Height 32½ in.; width 22¼ in. (0.83 x 0.57). Painted c. 1445.

FRA ANGELICO · Florentine 1387-1455

The Healing of Palladia by Saint Cosmas and Saint Damian

This variation of colour in uneven superficies, is what confounds an unskilful Painter; but if he takes care to mark the Out-lines of his Superficie and the seat of his lights in the manner I have before taught, he will find the true colouring no such difficult matter: for first he will alter the superficies properly as far as the line of separation, either with white or black sparingly as only with gentle dew; then he will in the same manner bedew the other side of the line, if I may be allow'd the expression, then this again, and so on by turns, till the light side is brightened with a more transparent colour, and the same colour on the other side dies away like smoak into an easy shade. But you shou'd always remember that no Superficie shou'd ever be made so white, that you cannot make it still brighter: even in Painting the whitest cloaths you shou'd abstain from coming near the strongest of that colour; because the Painter has nothing but white wherewith to imitate the polish of the most shining Superficie whatsoever, as I know of none but black, with which he can represent the utmost shade and obscurity of night. For this reason when he paints a white habit, he shou'd take one of the four kinds of colours that are clear and open; and so again in painting any black habit, let him use another extreme, but not absolute black, as for instance the colour of the sea where it is very deep, which is extremely dark. In a word this composition of black and white has so much power, that when practised with art and method, it is capable of representing in painting the Superficie either of gold or of silver, and even of the clearest glass. Those Painters therefore are greatly to be condemned, who make use of white immoderately, and of black without judgment; for which reason I cou'd wish that the Painters were obliged to buy their white at a greater price than the most costly gems, and that both white and black were to be made of those Pearls which *Cleopatrea* dissolved in vinegar; that they might be more chary of it: it wou'd make their works more graceful and come nearer to truth.

LEON BATTISTA ALBERTI
De Pictura (1435)

In this painting, as Alberti recommends, the whites are not pure white nor the blacks absolute black. A piece of drapery, for example, is modeled from deep shades of color in the depth of the fold to less intense and more transparent color at the top of the fold. Beginning about 1500, however, painters developed a tendency to ignore the fact that color "dies away like smoak into an easy shade" and made shadows brown or black instead of "the colour of the sea where it is very deep." This tendency finally evolved into the exaggerations which characterized fashionable painting in the last century, and which provoked Whistler's remark: "Lights have been heightened until the white of the tube alone remains — shadows have been deepened until black alone is left" (see page 82). Collections: Lord Northwick, Thirlestaine House, near Cheltenham, Gloucestershire; Albert Keller, New York. *Samuel H. Kress Collection,* 1939. Wood. Height 14¼ in.; width 18¼ in. (0.36 x 0.46). Painted between 1438 and 1440 if, as most critics assume, it originally formed a part of the predella of the altarpiece which Fra Angelico painted at this time for the high altar of the church of San Marco, Florence.

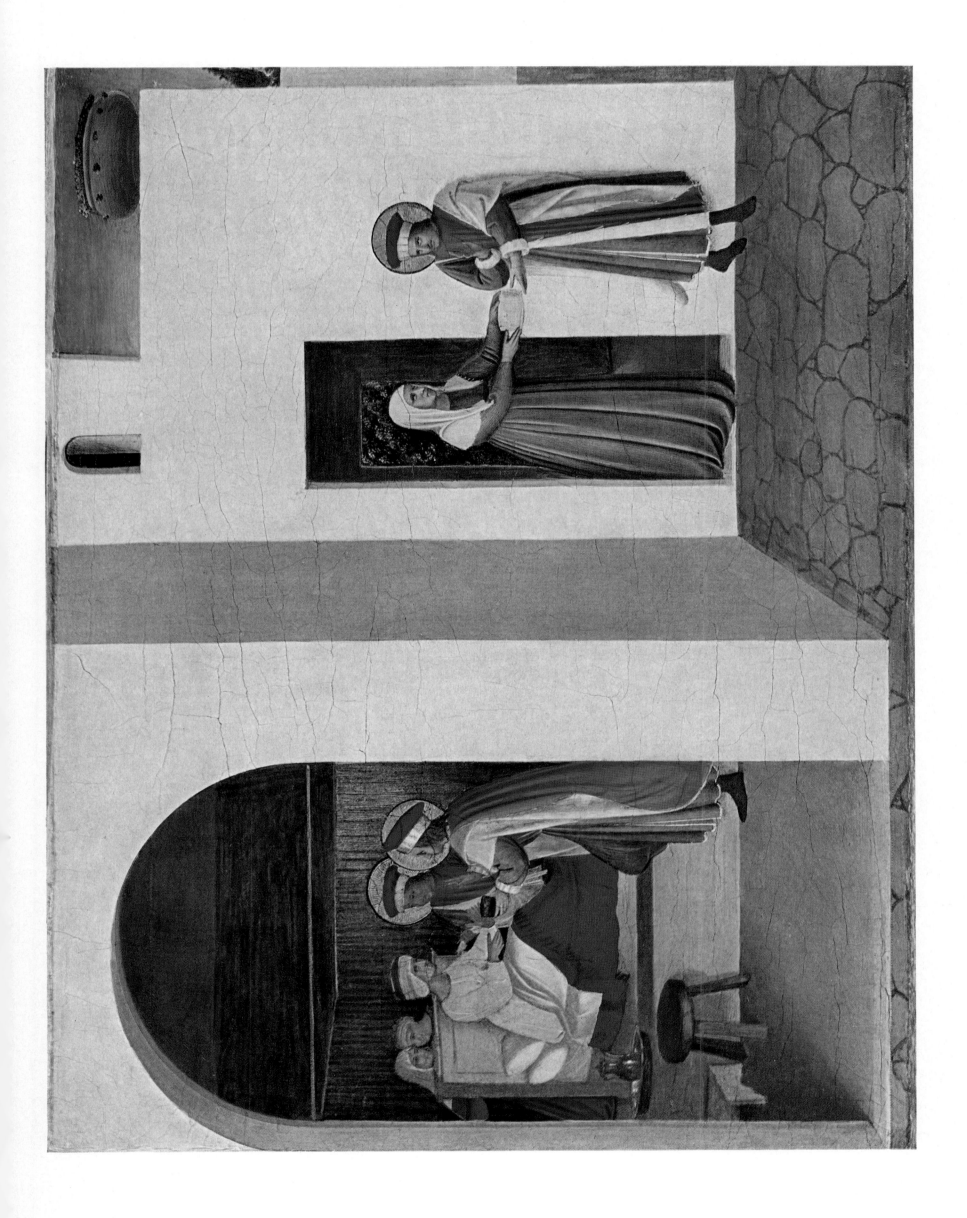

FRA FILIPPO LIPPI · Florentine c. 1406-1469

Madonna and Child

And between spiritual emotion and sensuous form
the same living compact maketh our Art, wherein
material appearances engage the soul's depth;
and if in men untrain'd without habit of thought
the ear is more æsthetic than the eye is, this cometh
from thatt sense being the earlier endow'd in animals
who, tho' they be all vacant in a picture-gallery
nor see themselves in a mirror, attend to music
and yield to fascination or vague wonder thereat.
So if we, changing Plato's old difficult term,
should rename his Ideas Influences, ther is none
would miss his meaning nor, by nebulous logic,
wish to refute his doctrin that indeed ther are
eternal Essences that exist in themselves,
supreme efficient causes of the thoughts of men.

What is Beauty? saith my sufferings then.—I answer
the lover and poet in my loose alexandrines:
Beauty is the highest of all these occult influences,
the quality of appearances that thru' the sense
wakeneth spiritual emotion in the mind of man:
And Art, as it createth new forms of beauty,
awakeneth new ideas that advance the spirit
in the life of Reason to the wisdom of God.
But highest Art must be rare as nativ faculty is,
and her surprise of magic winneth favor of men
more than her inspiration.

ROBERT BRIDGES
The Testament of Beauty (1929)

Fra Filippo Lippi set himself the task of finding a new "quality of appearances," which Bridges argues lies at the root of all art. Unlike most earlier painters, he selected as models the everyday people of Florence. As Berenson says (*Florentine Painters*, 1896): "His real place is with the genre painters; only his genre was of the soul, as that of others — of Benozzo Gozzoli, for example — was of the body." Thus his figures, though less idealized, are no less religious in feeling than the more formalized Madonnas and saints of Masolino and Domenico Veneziano. Collections: Solly, London; Kaiser Friedrich Museum, Berlin. *Samuel H. Kress Collection*, 1939. Wood. Height 31⅜ in.; width 20⅛ in. (0.80 x 0.51). Painted c. 1435-40.

FRA FILIPPO LIPPI · FLORENTINE c. 1406-1469

Saint Benedict Orders Saint Maurus to the Rescue of Saint Placidus

I am poor brother Lippo, by your leave!
You need not clap your torches to my face.
Zooks, what 's to blame? you think you see a monk!
What, 't is past midnight, and you go the rounds,
And here you catch me at an alley's end
Where sportive ladies leave their doors ajar? . . .
Here 's spring come, and the nights one makes up bands
To roam the town and sing out carnival,
And I've been three weeks shut within my mew,
A-painting for the great man, saints and saints
And saints again. . . .
You should not take a fellow eight years old
And make him swear to never kiss the girls. . . .
For me, I think I speak as I was taught;
I always see the garden and God there
A-making man's wife: and, my lesson learned,
The value and significance of flesh,
I can't unlearn ten minutes afterwards. . . .

Your hand, sir, and good-by: no lights, no lights!
The street 's hushed, and I know my own way back,
Don't fear me! There 's the gray beginning. Zooks!

ROBERT BROWNING
Fra Lippo Lippi (1855)

Fra Filippo's tranquil scenes from the lives of the saints, although modeled to a considerable degree on everyday people, as pointed out in the preceding note, give no indication of his turbulent private life. Browning's poem, based on Vasari, describes how Fra Filippo Lippi was shut up in a room by his great patron, Cosimo de' Medici, who wished him to complete a certain painting. Unable to endure this confinement, Fra Filippo let himself down from the window with a rope made of bed sheets, and roamed the streets of Florence seeking amusement. He is also said to have seduced a nun, who later became his wife. The present representation of the miraculous rescue of a monk who has fallen into a lake while filling his pitcher is characteristic of the narrative scenes often used to decorate the base, or predella, of an altarpiece. In this case the altar may have been the one with scenes from the lives of Saint Benedict and Saint Bernard which Vasari recorded as having been painted by Fra Filippo for the nuns of the Murate, Florence. Collections: Cernuschi; Édouard Aynard, Lyons. *Samuel H. Kress Collection*, 1939. Wood. Height 16⅜ in.; width 28 in. (0.415 x 0.71). Painted probably c. 1445.

BOTTICELLI · FLORENTINE 1444-1510
Portrait of a Youth

In Buddhism and other Oriental religions, all of which have strong tendencies to mysticism, hands play a large part in solemnities. The whole system of the mudras, or position of hands, in Buddhism is as complex as mysterious, which with its infinite combinations, positions of hands, their turnings, knittings of fingers and so on, serves to indicate innumerable gods and goddesses who are nothing less than the personification of different moods of the human mind. . . . All this probably came from India, where the cult of the hand and foot seems to have been always cherished. There are innumerable representations of hands, both beautiful and ugly, always very symbolic, in Indian Art and its derivatives in the Art of all Eastern lands. . . . Maple-leaves are called in Japan 'human hands,' because of their similarity in form, but I would say more, that those young pale leaves, extending in late spring, expanding visibly after sun and rain, are like the dancing hands of children. If young buds are signs of the mystery of expanding life, young hands are as well. . . .

If we trace the evolution of Botticelli's art, taking into consideration this inner development, it would appear to be of this nature: at first he was too exclusively occupied with the outward aspect of the hand and its technical difficulties; then his spiritual sense awoke; but being strictly dependent upon the still tenacious realism, its expression was at first what I called the 'characteristic,' the expression of the soul or its intentions immediately behind the exterior. And then, as his art approached more and more to its absolute domain, his outward form being gradually released from the grip of realism, the expression was also released from the immediate illustration of the character of the actual person represented, and became freer, finally arriving at symbolism, just as the outward form became a linear design. If in the outward form Botticelli's great merit lay in the linear, so in spiritual expression it must lie in the corresponding one, the symbolic. . . .

Thus, psychologically, Botticelli's hand developed. At the end of this study, let us admire the finest hand ever painted by him, in which, I may say, all the qualities I have mentioned were perfectly combined. I mean the hand of the [Portrait of a Youth]. It is the hand of an Adonis, where the soft feminine charm is mingled with a man's strength, though still young. It is a perfect hand. Except in a few of El Greco's masterpieces, you cannot see such a hand, a mere hand, with a whole mystery behind it.

YUKIO YASHIRO
Sandro Botticelli (1925)

Whether paintings like the one reproduced can be considered portraits at all is doubtful. They present, rather, ideal types of adolescent beauty. Yashiro points out that in looking at portraits by Botticelli: "Your interest in the persons represented is very slight. . . . Rather you are immersed in a vague ideal atmosphere, which floats above the individualistic world." Collections: Louis, Comte de Pourtalès-Gorgier, Paris; Baron Arthur de Schickler, Martinvast, France; Comtesse Hubert de Pourtalès (his daughter); Mackay, Roslyn, New York. *Mellon Collection,* 1937. Wood. Height 16¼ in.; width 12½ in. (0.412 x 0.318). Painted 1483-84.

SASSETTA · SIENESE 1392-1450

Saint Anthony Distributing His Wealth to the Poor

Now whilst he was meditating . . . . the Lesson was being read, and at the end of all [the passages from] the Scriptures, the Gospel was read, and he heard our Lord Who said unto the rich man, "If thou wishest to be perfect, go and sell everything which thou hast, and give to the poor, and take thy cross, and come after Me, and there shall be unto thee treasure in heaven." And the blessed Anthony received the word of the Gospel as a sign, and he reflected that this reading had not taken place as a matter of chance, but in order that the righteous idea which had taken up its abode in him might be confirmed. And straightway he went out from the church, and departed and set in order his house and the possessions which he had inherited from his parents. Now he had three hundred fields, a great estate [which produced] abundant crops, and these he remitted to the people of his village, so that they might trouble neither himself nor his sister; but the remainder of his other possessions which were in the house he sold, and gathered in money not a little, which he distributed among the poor, but he laid by a little which was sufficient for his sister's wants.

And when, on another First Day of the week, he had again entered the church at the time of [the reading of] the Gospel, he inclined his ear carefully to see what word would come forth for him; and as he was inclining his ear the word of our Lord to His disciples was immediately read out, saying, "Take no thought for the morrow." And straightway he received the commandment readily, and he went out and distributed that which remained to him for his sister among the poor. Now unto his sister he spake words of love, and of truth, and of the fear of God, and he made her mind to be after the manner of his own; and he delivered her over to certain chaste nuns who were to be found at that time. And when he had made an end of these things he forthwith became a solitary monk, and he took no care for anything whatsoever except his soul, and he began to train himself in the strictest abstinence and self-denial.

ATHANASIUS
The Life of Saint Anthony (c. 4th Century after Christ)

Naturalism in Italian painting increased throughout the fourteenth century until most traces of the Byzantine style had disappeared. In the early decades of the fifteenth century late Gothic art flowered particularly in Siena in such enchanting paintings as the one reproduced. In spite of medieval characteristics noticeable in the dual representatition of the Saint, descending the stairs and distributing alms, Sassetta is as advanced as any painter of his age in his sensitive appreciation of the relation between architecture and figures. One of the most poetic of narrative artists, he has told in a series of small panels, four of which are in the National Gallery of Art, the legend of Saint Anthony Abbot. The present painting, the second of the series, illustrates the scene described above by Athanasius. Other extant panels now accepted as belonging to the series are: Saint Anthony at Mass, in the Kaiser Friedrich Museum, Berlin; Saint Anthony Leaving His Monastery, National Gallery of Art, Samuel H. Kress Collection; The Temptation of Saint Anthony, and Saint Anthony and the Devils, both in the Jarves Collection, Yale University, New Haven; Saint Anthony and the Porringer, Lehman Collection, New York; The Meeting of Saint Anthony and Saint Paul, and The Obsequies of Saint Anthony, both in the National Gallery of Art, Samuel H. Kress Collection. Collections: Nevin, Rome; Dan Fellows Platt, Englewood, New Jersey. *Samuel H. Kress Collection*, 1939. Wood. Height 18⅝ in.; width 13⅝ in. (0.475 x 0.345). Painted c. 1436.

GIOVANNI DI PAOLO · Sienese 1403-1482

The Annunciation

The germ of Giovanni di Paolo's stylistic growth was a vivid imagination inflamed by a deeply religious temperament. Emotional stress was not uncommon at the time. The revivalism of S. Bernardino was achieved by simple descriptive methods. A comparable directness gives Giovanni di Paolo's pictures their peculiar mystical intensity. The religious mystic is a person who, gifted with a literal faith in events or dogmas too far outside the range of the experience of the ordinary individual to be generally credible in a literal sense, goes on to endow with a symbolist significance concepts he had at first accepted as simple facts. Giovanni di Paolo's realism and super-realism seem to argue an emotional conviction of this literal, yet transcendental nature.

That literary painting has its peculiar validity we cannot doubt. The twin elements of form and narrative in the finite work of art are susceptible of individual extension to an infinite degree. We can conceive of some paintings whose form is so subtilised that the spectator is unconscious of emotional deficiencies, and of others so direct and so passionate that he ignores their fundamental formal incoherence. Giovanni di Paolo is one of the few Italian painters to have created a convincing and original imaginative world. As he emerged from the predominantly æsthetic orbit of Sassetta, the force of his own disposition slowly compelled him to transcribe his imaginative impressions with decreasing reference to æsthetic dictates. When we remember that at the end of his life he was working in competition with Matteo di Giovanni, Benvenuto di Giovanni and Neroccio dei Landi, painters whose object for the most part was a merely æsthetic appeal, the nonconformist character of his style appears most striking. Giovanni di Paolo was a Gerard Hopkins in a world of Swinburnes. He is often grotesque and sometimes rude. But his faults are the expression of an inner strain few other painters felt, and his pictures at their best provide us with a unique example of style heated to receive the impress of a vital and candescent personality.

JOHN POPE-HENNESSY
Giovanni di Paolo (1938)

The theme of the painting is the Fall and Redemption of Man, with Joseph and Mary shown as the counterparts of Adam and Eve. Saint Joseph is an unusual figure in scenes of the Annunciation (see Shapiro, *Art Bulletin*, 1945). His appearance here may perhaps be explained by the sudden growth of his cult during the first half of the fifteenth century. It is significant that he warms his hands before a golden fire. "Since fire is the most noble element, its virtue is wonderfully diffused," wrote Berchorius a century before this picture was painted. "For fire lurks secretly in all things, as is evident when two solid bodies are struck together, for then the fire breaks out, though it was not at all believed to be hidden there. Thus God is truly in all things, though invisible. . . . Indeed, we may well speak of the fire of charity, or the fire of the Holy Spirit, and especially of the fire of divine love, which is in many people who are not believed to possess it" (see Miess, *Art Bulletin*, 1945). The panel belonged to a predella, other parts of which are: The Nativity, in the Vatican Gallery; The Crucifixion, in the Kaiser Friedrich Museum, Berlin; The Presentation in the Temple, in the Metropolitan Museum, New York; and The Adoration of the Magi, in the Cleveland Museum. Collections: Benson, London. *Samuel H. Kress Collection,* 1939. Wood. Height 15¾ in.; width 18¼ in. (0.40 x 0.465). Painted 1440-45.

FRANCESCO DI GIORGIO · Sienese 1439-1502

God the Father Surrounded by Angels and Cherubim

I struck the board, and cry'd, No more.
I will abroad.
What? shall I ever sigh and pine?
My lines and life are free; free as the rode,
Loose as the winde, as large as store.
Shall I be still in suit?
Have I no harvest but a thorn
To let me bloud, and not restore
What I have lost with cordiall fruit?
Sure there was wine
Before my sighs did drie it: there was corn
Before my tears did drown it.
Is the yeare onely lost to me?
Have I no bayes to crown it?
No flowers, no garlands gay? all blasted?
All wasted?
Not so, my heart: but there is fruit,
And thou hast hands.
Recover all thy sigh-blown age
On double pleasures: leave thy cold dispute
Of what is fit, and not. Forsake thy cage,
Thy rope of sands,
Which pettie thoughts have made, and made to thee
Good cable, to enforce and draw,
And be thy law,
While thou didst wink and wouldst not see.
Away; take heed:
I will abroad.
Call in thy deaths head there: tie up thy fears.
He that forbears
To suit and serve his need,
Deserves his load.
But as I rav'd and grew more fierce and wilde
At every word,
Me thoughts I heard one calling, *Child!*
And I reply'd, *My Lord.*

GEORGE HERBERT
The Temple (1633)

What could illustrate more aptly George Herbert's poem than Francesco di Giorgio's picture? God the Father seems to speak, while far below the poet answers. Both painting and poem pay a mystical tribute to the irresistible power of the Word of God in the divine and the natural order. Originally Francesco di Giorgio's panel probably formed the upper part of a painting of the Nativity. The complicated foreshortening of the figures is a tour de force equaled only in the work of the most advanced artists of the time, painters like Mantegna and Melozzo da Forlì. Francesco di Giorgio was famous in the fifteenth century primarily as a sculptor and an architect. His work in these arts shows the same spontaneity and brilliance apparent in his rare paintings. Collections: Alphonse Kann, Paris; Philip Lehman, New York. *Samuel H. Kress Collection*, 1939. Wood. Oval. Height 14⅜ in.; width 20⅜ in. (0.365 x 0.52). Painted c. 1470.

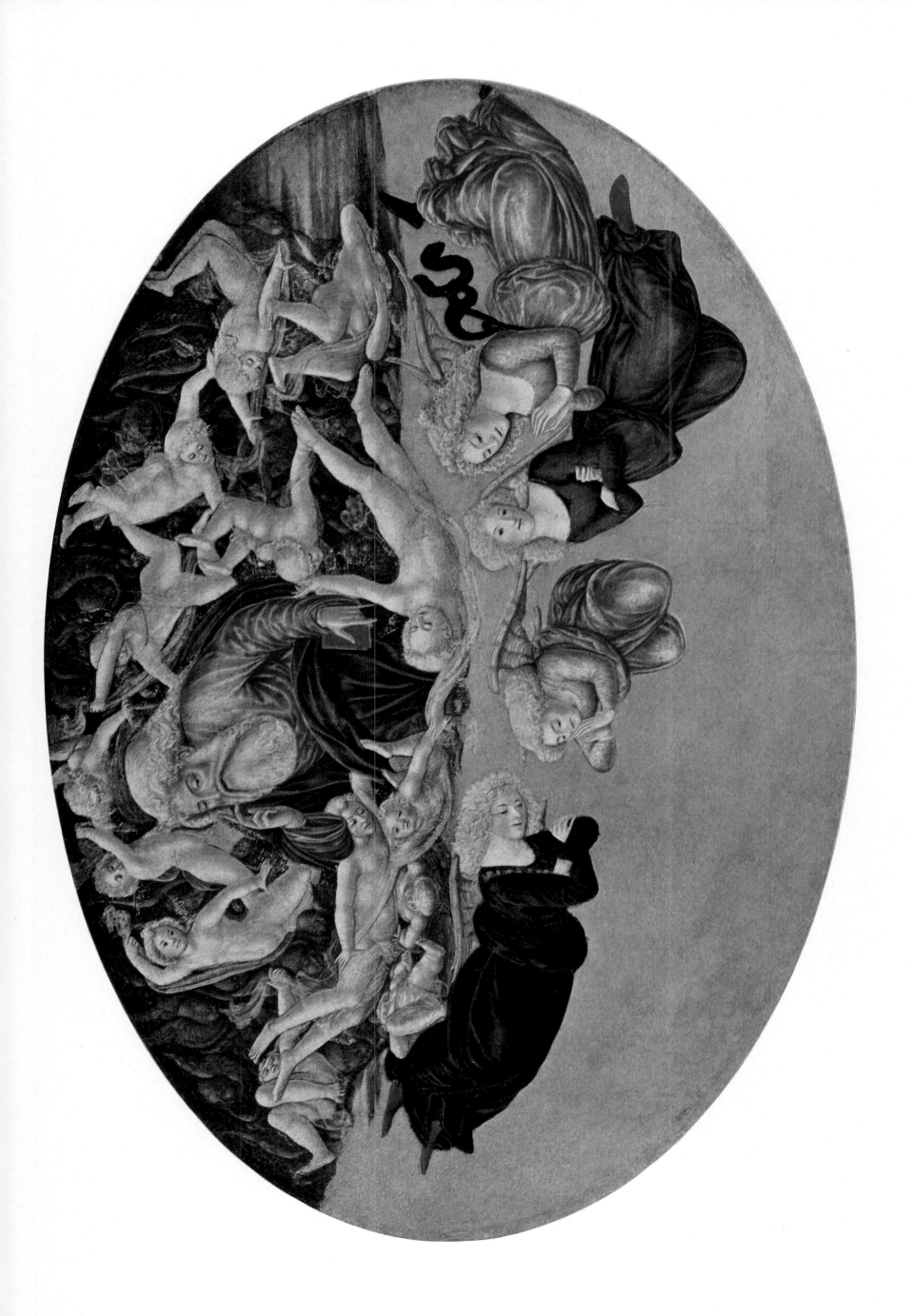

FILIPPINO LIPPI · Florentine 1457-1504

Tobias and the Angel

In fact, the poet who treats a well-known story or a well-known character, has already made considerable progress towards his object. He can afford to pass over a hundred cold details, which would otherwise be indispensable to the understanding of his whole; and the more quickly his audience comprehends this, the sooner their interest will be awakened. This advantage the painter also enjoys, when his subject is not new to us, and we recognize, at the first glance, the intention and meaning of his whole composition; at once not only see that his characters are speaking, but hear what they are saying. The most important effect depends on the first glance.

Gotthold Ephraim Lessing
Laokoon (1766)

Painting is the noblest of the arts. In it are summed up all the sensations. In its presence each person can, as his imagination wishes, create his special story. With a single glance of the eye his soul can be invaded by the most profound recollections. It requires no effort of memory; everything is summarized in an instant.— Painting is the perfect art that encompasses and completes all the others.

Like music, it acts on the soul through the intermediary of tones, its harmonious colors corresponding to the harmonies of sounds; but in painting a unity is obtained that is not possible in music, where the chords follow one another and the judgment experiences an incessant fatigue if it would unite the end and the beginning. In short, the ear is an inferior sense to the eye. The hearing can grasp but a single sound at a time, while the sight takes in everything, simplifying in accordance with its wishes.

Like literature, the art of painting is able to state what it intends, with this advantage, that the *reader* knows immediately the prelude, development and outcome. Literature and music demand an effort of memory in order to appreciate the whole. . . . You can dream freely when you listen to music as well as when you look at a painting; but in reading a book you are a slave to the ideas of the author. The writer is obliged to address himself to the intelligence before he can move the heart, and God knows that a reasoned sensation is not very strong.

The sight alone produces an instantaneous impulse.

Paul Gauguin
Notes synthétiques de Paul Gauguin (1910)

The story of Tobias and the Angel was one of the most familiar themes of Renaissance painting. It was undoubtedly popular with parents of absent sons, emphasizing as it did both filial piety and divine protection. Tobias, according to the Book of Tobit, was guided by the Archangel Raphael to the banks of the river Tigris where a great fish which leaped out of the water furnished, along with other miraculous aid, the cure for the blindness of Tobias' father. In Filippino Lippi's panel not only are the central facts of the story told, but the mood of sheltering divinity is conveyed, thus achieving the wholeness of which Gauguin speaks. Collections: Benson, London. *Samuel H. Kress Collection*, 1939. Wood. Height 12⅞ in.; width 9¼ in. (0.325 x 0.235). Painted c. 1475-80.

FILIPPINO LIPPI · FLORENTINE 1457-1504

Portrait of a Youth

The plot then is the first principle and as it were the soul of tragedy: character comes second. It is much the same also in painting; if a man smeared a canvas with the loveliest colours at random, it would not give as much pleasure as an outline in black and white. . . .

Moreover, in everything that is beautiful, whether it be a living creature or any organism composed of parts, these parts must not only be orderly arranged but must also have a certain magnitude of their own; for beauty consists in magnitude and ordered arrangement. From which it follows that neither would a very small creature be beautiful — for our view of it is almost instantaneous and therefore confused — nor a very large one, since being unable to view it all at once, we lose the effect of a single whole; for instance, suppose a creature a thousand miles long. As then creatures and other organic structures must have a certain magnitude and yet be easily taken in by the eye, so too with plots. . . .

Poetry tends to give general truths while history gives particular facts. . . .

We must copy the good portrait-painters who, while rendering the distinctive form and making a likeness, yet paint people better than they are. It is the same with the poet. . . .

Obviously the art which makes its appeal to everybody is eminently vulgar.

ARISTOTLE
Poetics (4th Century B.C.)

In sensitive expression of the beauty of adolescence, Renaissance Florence is the closest rival of classical Greece. Filippino Lippi has attained this expression through the happy balance between imitation and idealization recommended by Aristotle for portraiture, a balance between achieving a likeness and painting "people better than they are." A number of Florentine portraits similar to the one reproduced have been preserved, and it is often difficult to attribute them with certainty. The present picture has been ascribed to Botticelli, but in view of its similarity to the portraits of the young men in the Brancacci chapel known to have been painted by Filippino Lippi, its attribution to him seems more likely. For other views on portraiture, see pages 40, 52, 66, 90 and 96. Collections: Liechtenstein Gallery, Vienna; Frank D. Stout, Chicago. *Mellon Collection,* 1937. Wood. Height 20 in.; width 13⅞ in. (0.51 x 0.355). Painted c. 1485.

LUCA SIGNORELLI · Umbrian c. 1441-1523

Eunostos of Tanagra

Who was the hero Eunostus in Tanagra, and why may no women enter his grove?

Eunostus was the son of Elieus, who was the son of Cephisus, and Scias. They relate that he acquired his name because he was brought up by the nymph Eunosta. Handsome and righteous as he was, he was no less virtuous and ascetic. They say that Ochnê, his cousin, one of the daughters of Colonus, became enamoured of him; but when Eunostus repulsed her advances and, after upbraiding her, departed to accuse her to her brothers, the maiden forestalled him by doing this very thing against him. She incited her brothers, Echemus, Leon, and Bucolus, to kill Eunostus, saying that he had consorted with her by force. They, accordingly, lay in ambush for the young man and slew him. Then Elieus put them in bonds; but Ochnê repented, and was filled with trepidation and, wishing to free herself from the torments caused by her love, and also feeling pity for her brothers, reported the whole truth to Elieus, and he to Colonus. And when Colonus had given judgement, Ochnê's brothers were banished, and she threw herself from a precipice, as Myrtis, the lyric poetess of Anthedon, has related.

But the shrine and the grove of Eunostus were so strictly guarded against entry and approach by women that, often, when earthquakes or droughts or other signs from heaven occurred, the people of Tanagra were wont to search diligently and to be greatly concerned lest any woman might have approached the place undetected; and some relate, among them Cleidamus, a man of prominence, that Eunostus met them on his way to the sea to bathe because a woman had set foot within the sacred precinct. And Diocles also, in his treatise upon the *Shrines of Heroes,* quotes a decree of the people of Tanagra concerning the matters which Cleidamus reported.

Plutarch

Moralia (1st or 2nd Century after Christ)

This panel, one of a series devoted to the heroes and heroines of antiquity, was painted for the decoration of a palace probably in Siena. Other figures from the same room now preserved in various museums are: Alexander the Great, Tiberius Gracchus, Claudia Quinta, Scipio Africanus and Sulpicia. It was a favorite decorative scheme of the early Renaissance to represent on the walls exemplars of classical virtue. The striking features of Signorelli's figure, the nervousness of its silhouette, the austerity of its design, the aloofness of its conception, are typical. He discarded all the minor charms of painting "in his resolution to express high thought and tragic passion by pure form," to quote John Addington Symonds, *Renaissance in Italy,* 1877. Collections: Earl of Ashburnham, Ashburnham Place, Battle, Sussex; Lord Northampton, Castle Ashby, Northampton; Édouard Kann, Paris. *Samuel H. Kress Collection*, 1939. Wood. Height 37⅞ in.; width 20⅝ in. (0.885 x 0.525). Painted c. 1495-1500.

PERUGINO · Umbrian c. 1445-1523

The Crucifixion with the Virgin and Saints

Crucifixion! This is the word upon which we must meditate today. For is it not Good Friday?

You desire to know the art of living, my friend?
It is contained in one phrase: make use of suffering.

Will you now reject suffering as vain, useless, fierce, tyrannical, when formerly you were able to draw from it a moral and a benefit? To damn it is easier than to bless it, but it means falling back into the point of view of earthly, carnal, natural man. How else did Christianity conquer the world but by the deification of grief, by the glorious transmutation of anguish into triumph, of the crown of thorns into a crown of glory, and of a gallows into a symbol of salvation? What signifies the apotheosis of the cross, if not the death of death, the destruction of sin, the beatification of the martyr, the raising to heaven of voluntary sacrifice, the defiance of pain?

"O Death, where is thy sting? O Grave, where is thy victory?" From a long contemplation of this theme — the agony of the Just, peace in the midst of agony, and glory in such peace — mankind came to understand that a new religion had been born, that is, a new way of explaining life and of understanding suffering. . . .

Crucify the ungovernable self, mortify yourself wholly, offer up everything to God, and peace which is not of this world will descend upon you. For eighteen centuries no greater word has been spoken, and although men seek an ever more exact, more complete application of justice, yet secretly they put their faith in pardon only, for only pardon conciliates the inviolable purity of perfection with the infinite pity for weakness.

Henri Frédéric Amiel
Journal intime (April 15, 1870)

Few paintings convey more clearly than this the concepts of "peace in the midst of agony," "the inviolable purity of perfection," and "the infinite pity for weakness." Though Vasari said Perugino was a person of little religion and disbelieved in the immortality of the soul, to an extraordinary degree he makes us vibrate to the emotions of the religious themes he illustrates. The present triptych was formerly ascribed to Perugino's greater pupil, Raphael, but as we know that it was given to the Church of San Domenico at San Gimignano by Bartolommeo Bartoli, who died in 1497, when Raphael was only fourteen, we can be certain that this attribution was incorrect. The picture is now unanimously attributed to Perugino. Collections: Church of San Domenico, San Gimignano; Hermitage Gallery, Leningrad. *Mellon Collection*, 1937. Transferred from wood to canvas. Center panel, height 39⅞ in.; width 22¼ in. (1.015 x 0.565). Each side panel, height 37½ in.; width 12 in. (0.95 x 0.305). Painted c. 1485.

RAPHAEL · Umbrian 1483-1520

The Niccolini-Cowper Madonna

"Beauty is a thing severe and unapproachable, never to be won by a languid lover. You must lie in wait for her coming and take her unawares, press her hard and clasp her in a tight embrace, and force her to yield. Form is a Proteus more intangible and more manifold than the Proteus of the legend; compelled, only after long wrestling, to stand forth manifest in his true aspect. Some of you are satisfied with the first shape, or at most by the second or the third that appears. Not thus wrestle the victors, the unvanquished painters who never suffer themselves to be deluded by all those treacherous shadow-shapes; they persevere till nature at the last stands bare to their gaze, and her very soul is revealed.

"In this manner worked Raphael," said the old man, taking off his cap to express his reverence for the King of Art. "His transcendent greatness came from the intimate sense that, in him, seems as if it would shatter external form. Form in his figures (as with us) is a symbol, a means of communicating sensations, ideas, the vast imaginings of a poet. Every face is a whole world."

HONORÉ DE BALZAC
Le Chef-d'œuvre inconnu (1831)

Great curiosity had been excited amongst the artists to see Zoffany's picture of the *Florentine Gallery,* which had been much spoken of by such of the English noblemen and gentlemen as (returned from abroad) had visited Florence in their continental tour. . . .

The painter in this piece . . . . has not neglected to introduce his own portrait . . . . He is exhibiting, to a group of *virtuosi,* a Madonna, by Raffael, which is introduced by way of episode, and a profitable one it turned out to the artist. The picture did not belong to the gallery—it was picked up by accident by Zoffany, and for a small sum. He was wont to ask all English comers to Florence, "Have you seen my Raffael?—Ah! den you must see it." He is herein submitting it to the admiring group, Sir John Dick, the Earl of Plymouth, Mr. Stevenson, the Earl of Dartmouth, and last, though the first *par eminence,* the late Earl Cowper, who, charmed with its *gusto,* purchased it, and brought it to England. It is now in the collection of the present worthy earl.

The picture is considered an original Raffael, and a treasure of art. His lordship paid down a certain liberal sum, and granted, by way of residue, an annuity of a hundred pounds, which the fortunate painter, (who lived, as is said and pretty generally believed, to be between ninety and a hundred,) enjoyed to the last. Hence this Madonna, perhaps, whatever may be its merits, is the dearest Raffael that ever was purchased, even by a travelling English lord!

The London Literary Gazette (July 15, 1826)

Collections: Casa Niccolini, Florence; John Zoffany, Florence; Earl Cowper and descendants, Panshanger, Hertfordshire. *Mellon Collection,* 1937. Wood. Height 31¾ in.; width 22⅝ in. (0.81 x 0.57). Painted 1508.

PISANELLO · Veronese c. 1395-1455

Profile Portrait of a Lady

Historically, the portrait, as Ruskin realized, is characteristic of certain periods which we call humanistic. In such periods man is the measure of all things, and all things are made to contribute to his awareness of his own vitality. Art is a tribute to man's own humanity. Such, no doubt, is the real basis of the popularity of portrait-painting. . . .

The rise of the portrait corresponds fairly exactly with the rise of the novel. Portraits of Dante and others have been identified in the fresco ascribed to Giotto in the chapel of the Bargello, in Florence, which may be as late as 1337; Boccaccio wrote his first tale in 1339, and his "Decameron" nine years later. And just as at first the portrait in painting was a flat profile, so the character in the early Italian novel was somewhat restricted in depth. One must not work the comparison too far: the novel, indeed, did not attain the psychological subtlety and precision already evident in portrait painting by the end of the fifteenth century until much later — perhaps not until the seventeenth century. But the general interest in character, common to both painting and the novel, was a continuous and rapid development from the early Renaissance, and still persists. . . .

Many portraits, however, are admittedly great works of art, so that we have to ask ourselves finally what is it that distinguishes a portrait which is a psychological document from a portrait which is a work of art? One might answer: simply the æsthetic values, meaning the formal relations of space and colour which constitute the structural organization of all works of art.

HERBERT READ
The Anatomy of Art (1931)

The panel reproduced is one of the mysteries of the history of painting. Its traditional attribution to Pisanello is doubtful, for the costume seems to be of the type fashionable at the Burgundian Court around 1410, twenty years earlier than Pisanello's known activity. Yet, if the panel is French, as Richter, Hill and Degenhart believe, then in quality and style it is unique among Northern portraits. In any case the sitter belongs to that international aristocracy which through the interweaving of dynastic marriages brought about an international style of art in the fourteenth and fifteenth centuries. For other views on portraiture, see pages 32, 52, 66, 90 and 96. Collections: de Villeroy, Paris; Mackay, Roslyn, New York. *Mellon Collection,* 1937. Wood. Height 20⅜ in.; width 14⅜ in. (0.52 x 0.365). Painted c. 1420.

COSIMO TURA · FERRARESE c. 1430-1495

Madonna and Child in a Garden

Of all holy men and women the Virgin was the most honored and the most loved. Art exalted her above all creatures, and conceived her as an eternal thought of God. . . .

Inside monastery walls the world was spiritualized by the habit of contemplation; realities trembled, dissolved, and evaporated in prayers. The perfumes which mounted from flowers were likened to virtues — modesty, charity, forgetfulness of self. Since he was always meditating on the Virgin, the monk saw her everywhere. The clear spring in the cloister was her purity. The high mountain which closed off the horizon was her grandeur. She was the springtime, coming adorned with a garland of flowers that was a garland of virtues. When the monk stepped out of the monastery all the magnificent things he saw about him were only diminished aspects of the beauty he contemplated in the Virgin. She was the field of grain nourishing within us the bread of eternity, she was the rainbow colored by a ray of God's evening, she was the star from which a drop of dew falls upon our interior aridity. . . .

Like the concept of the girl-Virgin, the grouping of the biblical emblems around Our Lady was also the slow growth of time. Long before, the liturgical writers had chosen the most beautiful biblical metaphors for the adornment of the offices of the Virgin. "Star of the sea," "closed garden," "rose without thorns"—all the lovely biblical phrases came to compose together the richest of ornaments, the most marvelous of diadems:

> *Botrus, uva, favus, hortus,*
> *Thalamus, triclinium.*
> *Arca, navis, aura, portus,*
> *Luna, lampas, atrium.*

> Grape and cluster, honey, garden,
> Marriage bed and banquet-room,
> Ark and ship and breeze and haven,
> Moon and lamp and coming home.

So reads the Missal of Evreux. All the missals convey the same mild music by whole columns of nouns: flowers, perfumes, precious metals, colors, honeycombs, all that is most delicious in nature. The most delicate poets of later times have not been more sensitive to the enchantment of words. Thus, the litanies of the Virgin, which, in their present form, did not appear until 1576, have a distant origin. These beautiful words were recited perhaps less for the sake of a specific prayer than for the solace the words alone brought to the heart.

ÉMILE MÂLE
L'Art religieux du XIIe au XVIIIe siècle (1949)

Cosimo Tura was a master of pattern, and from that point of view the present picture is pleasing when looked at in any position — right side up, sideways or upside down. Note the repetitive rhythm in the scrolls, the floral background and the wiry lines of the Virgin's robes. Contemporary documents tell of Tura's using an aromatic moss paste for relief decorations on gilded chests. In Ferrara this technique became very popular because of the resulting fragrance. It is possible that such a paste formed the scroll reliefs in the painting reproduced. Collections: Harold I. Pratt, New York. *Samuel H. Kress Collection*, 1939. Wood. Height 9⅛ in.; width 7⅛ in. (0.232 x 0.181). Painted c. 1460.

FRANCESCO DEL COSSA · FERRARESE c. 1435-1477

The Crucifixion

Who can blot out the Crosse, which th'instrument
Of God, dew'd on mee in the Sacrament?
Who can deny mee power, and liberty
To stretch mine armes, and mine owne Crosse to be?
Swimme, and at every stroake, thou art thy Crosse;
The Mast and yard make one, where seas do tosse;
Looke downe, thou spiest out Crosses in small things;
Looke up, thou seest birds rais'd on crossed wings;
All the Globes frame, and spheares, is nothing else
But the Meridians crossing Parallels.
Materiall Crosses then, good physicke bee,
But yet spirituall have chiefe dignity.
These for extracted chimique medicine serve,
And cure much better, and as well preserve;
Then are you your own physicke, or need none,
When Still'd, or purg'd by tribulation.
For when that Crosse ungrudg'd, unto you stickes,
Then are you to your selfe, a Crucifixe.
As perchance, Carvers do not faces make,
But that away, which hid them there, do take;
Let Crosses, soe, take what hid Christ in thee,
And be his image, or not his, but hee.

JOHN DONNE
The Crosse (c. 1615)

The stark intensity of meaning in Donne's poem is analogous to the almost brutal severity of Cossa's picture. To both poet and painter, the image of the Cross is a brand to be burned into the soul. This small tondo, according to a reconstruction plausibly proposed by Longhi, was at the peak of a great altarpiece painted by Cossa for San Petronio, Bologna. Thus it was the climactic point the eye would reach, beyond the images and episodes of the saints which were painted on the other panels. Collections: Costabili, Ferrara; Philip Lehman, New York. *Samuel H. Kress Collection,* 1939. Wood. Diameter 25⅛ in. (0.64). Painted 1470-75.

CARLO CRIVELLI · Venetian 1430/35-c. 1493

Madonna and Child Enthroned with Donor

Wherfor in laude, as I best can or may,
Of thee, and of the whyte lily flour
Which that thee bar, and is a mayde alway,
To telle a storie I wol do my labour;
Not that I may encresen hir honour;
For she hir-self is honour, and the rote
Of bountee, next hir sone, and soules bote.—

O moder mayde! o mayde moder free!
O bush unbrent, brenninge in Moyses sighte,
That ravisedest doun fro the deitee,
Thurgh thyn humblesse, the goost that in th'alighte,
Of whos vertu, whan he thyn herte lighte,
Conceived was the fadres sapience,
Help me to telle it in thy reverence!

Lady! thy bountee, thy magnificence,
Thy vertu, and thy grete humilitee
Ther may no tonge expresse in no science;
For som-tyme, lady, er men praye to thee,
Thou goost biforn of thy benignitee,
And getest us the light, thurgh thy preyere,
To gyden us un-to thy sone so dere.

My conning is so wayk, o blisful quene,
For to declare thy grete worthinesse,
That I ne may the weighte nat sustene,
But as a child of twelf monthe old, or lesse,
That can unnethes any word expresse,
Right so fare I, and therfor I yow preye,
Gydeth my song that I shal of yow seye.

GEOFFREY CHAUCER
The Canterbury Tales (c. 1387)

GLOSSARY: *bote*, salvation; *moder*, mother; *unbrent*, unburnt; *brenninge*, burning; *fadres*, parents; *biforn*, before; *unnethes*, scarcely.

Not only in stone, but also in simulated stone, religious art of the quattrocento teems with marine motifs. Their first use, of course, is decorative, but there is also a theological meaning. In the ancient world, the dolphin was thought to carry the soul to the Isles of the Blessed. Later the Greek word for fish, *ichthus*, came to stand as an anagram for Jesus Christ, God's Son, Saviour. Jonah's liberation from the inside of a fish was also considered a prefiguration of the Resurrection. The shells are emblems of pilgrimage. (See Friedmann, *Gazette des Beaux-Arts*, 1947.) Above the Madonna is written the plaintive cry of the tiny donor, "Do not forget me, Mother of God, Queen of Heaven"—a plea which is the implied refrain of Chaucer's poem. Longhi believes the painting formed the central panel of the polyptych executed c. 1470 for the church at Porto San Giorgio. The best general estimate of Crivelli's style is given by Berenson (*Venetian Painters*, 1894): "He takes rank with the most genuine artists of all times and countries, and does not weary even when 'great masters' grow tedious. He expresses with the freedom and spirit of Japanese design a piety as wild and tender as Jacopo da Todi's, a sweetness of emotion as sincere and dainty as of a Virgin and Child carved in ivory by a French craftsman of the fourteenth century. The mystic beauty of Simone Martini, the agonized compassion of the young Bellini, are embodied by Crivelli in forms which have the strength of line and the metallic lustre of old Satsuma or lacquer, and which are no less tempting to the touch." Collections: Earl of Dudley, Himley Hall, Dudley; Cook, Richmond, Surrey. *Samuel H. Kress Collection*, 1939. Wood. Height 51 in.; width 21⅜ in. (1.295 x 0.545). Painted c. 1470.

ANTONELLO DA MESSINA · Sicilian 1430-1479

Madonna and Child

Wild air, world-mothering air,
Nestling me everywhere,
That each eyelash or hair
Girdles; goes home betwixt
The fleeciest, frailest-flixed
Snowflake; that 's fairly mixed
With, riddles, and is rife
In every least thing's life;
This needful, never spent,
And nursing element;
My more than meat and drink,
My meal at every wink;
This air, which, by life's law,
My lung must draw and draw
Now but to breathe its praise,
Minds me in many ways
Of her who not only
Gave God's infinity
Dwindled to infancy
Welcome in womb and breast,
Birth, milk, and all the rest
But mothers each new grace
That does now reach our race —
Mary Immaculate,

Merely a woman, yet
Whose presence, power is
Great as no goddess's
Was deemèd, dreamèd; who
This one work has to do —
Let all God's glory through,
God's glory which would go
Through her and from her flow
Off, and no way but so. . . .

Be thou then, O thou dear
Mother, my atmosphere;
My happier world, wherein
To wend and meet no sin;
Above me, round me lie
Fronting my froward eye
With sweet and scarless sky;
Stir in my ears, speak there
Of God's love, O live air,
Of patience, penance, prayer:
World-mothering air, air wild,
Wound with thee, in thee isled,
Fold home, fast fold thy child.

GERARD MANLEY HOPKINS
Mary Mother of Divine Grace Compared to the Air we Breathe (1883)

According to Vasari, Antonello studied in Bruges and was the first painter to introduce the Flemish oil technique into Italy. Though oil painting was practiced in Italy before his time, as is now known, Antonello attained unusual mastery of the technique. Transparent oil glazes, more suited to the rendering of light effects than is tempera alone, give this painting an extraordinary luminosity, a sense of pure atmosphere, the "world-mothering air" which Gerard Manley Hopkins refers to in his poem. Collections: William Graham, London; Benson, London; Mackay, Roslyn, New York. *Mellon Collection,* 1937. Wood. Height 23¼ in.; width 17¼ in. (0.59 x 0.44). Painted probably 1475, shortly after Antonello's arrival in Venice from his native Sicily.

VITTORE CARPACCIO · Venetian c. 1455-1523/26

A Saint Reading

Like the good primitive that he still was, Carpaccio told all that he knew in each one of his canvases. It is true that he knew much. One may love him for his anecdotes, for he is a wonderful story-teller. But the anecdote, always transfigured and magnified, always a motive for painted decorations and transpositions, is lost in the poetic sentiment which lifts up and frees everything. The sea is covered with boats and with ships. The city is as exact and new as that which Bellini paints, but more somber harmonies announce its maturity. Through their high arcades, the palaces permit us to see masts with pennants flying from them, the multicolored pavements of the great docks where merchants and promenaders come and go before the vessels at anchor. We see also leprous houses, dirty clothes hung from one façade to the other across the plague-ridden canals, and the incredible swarm of beggars, boatmen, jugglers, and ruffians. There are people everywhere: in the streets, on the staircases, on the bridges, and on the terraces. Lords and ladies file by, people are chatting, people are parading, people bend the knee before princes who receive in the open air. Palm trees grow in solitary squares, an unexpected camel is seen outlined at the corner of a dock, and the lion of Saint Jerome actually treads the pavement of the Piazzetta dragged along by a black lion-tamer around whom the street boys dance gayly. Carpaccio mingles with the crowd, he listens, he gossips, he is out of doors all day long. The violins and the brass instruments of the showmen creak and snore; the showman's nasal patter excites jest and laughter. The good painter is in the very first rank. Everything amuses him, but if one keeps one's eye upon him one sees why his face becomes serious at times. In some corner he has seen a strange isolated figure which holds his attention. . . . He becomes pensive and turns aside, the sound of the music dies away.

ÉLIE FAURE
Histoire de l'art (1921)

It is such isolated figures as this in Carpaccio's crowded scenes that elevate his paintings above the prose of genre. In the present case there is evidence that the picture is a fragment of a larger composition. While the painting was in the Benson Collection, a small arm and foot, corresponding to those of a Christ Child, were visible against the cushion to the left, and slight traces of these details can still be seen. The same seated figure appears in the guise of a midwife in the Birth of the Virgin ascribed to Carpaccio and assistants, in the Carrara Academy, Bergamo. Collections: Marquis of Exeter, Lincolnshire; Benson, London. *Samuel H. Kress Collection*, 1939. Wood. Height 30¾ in.; width 20 in. (0.78 x 0.51). Painted c. 1500.

GIOVANNI BELLINI · Venetian c. 1430-1516

Portrait of a Young Man in Red

The artist must imitate that which is within the thing, that which is active through form and figure, and discourses to us by symbols — the *Natur-geist,* or spirit of nature, as we unconsciously imitate those whom we love; for so only can he hope to produce any work truly natural in the object and truly human in the effect. The idea which puts the form together cannot itself be the form. It is above form, and is its essence, the universal in the individual, or the individuality itself, — the glance and the exponent of the indwelling power. . . .

Hence a good portrait is the abstract of the personal; it is not the likeness for actual comparison, but for recollection. This explains why the likeness of a very good portrait is not always recognized; because some persons never abstract, and amongst these are especially to be numbered the near relations and friends of the subject, in consequence of the constant pressure and check exercised on their minds by the actual presence of the original.

SAMUEL TAYLOR COLERIDGE
Biographia Literaria (1817)

The quotation above defines the problem of portraiture. In the Renaissance, "near relations and friends" seem to have accepted more readily than today "the abstract of the personal." Consequently, from that period we have received a series of great portraits which show "the universal in the individual," but which remain, because of their abstractions, difficult to identify, even when it seems likely that they represent famous personages. Borenius (*Burlington Magazine,* 1932) has pointed out that the present picture resembles a seventeenth-century drawing of a portrait once in the Vendramin Collection, Venice. The sitter was perhaps a member of that celebrated Venetian family. For other views on portraiture, see pages 32, 40, 66, 90 and 96. Collections: Von Ingenheim, Ober-Rengersdorf, Germany. *Mellon Collection,* 1937. Wood. Height 12½ in.; width 10¾ in. (0.32 x 0.265). Painted c. 1480.

GIOVANNI BELLINI · VENETIAN c. 1430-1516

Orpheus

Orpheus with his Lute made Trees,
And the Mountaine tops that freeze,
Bow themselues when he did sing.
To his Musicke, Plants and Flowers
Euer sprung, as Sunne and Showers,
There had made a lasting Spring.
Euery thing that heard him play,
Euen the Billowes of the Sea,
Hung their heads, & then lay by.
In sweet Musicke is such Art,
Killing care, & griefe of heart,
Fall asleepe, or hearing dye.

WILLIAM SHAKESPEARE
The Life of King Henry the Eight (1623)

The old masters taught, not because they liked teaching, nor yet from any idea of serving the cause of art, nor yet because they were paid to teach by the parents of their pupils. The parents probably paid no money at first. The masters took pupils and taught them because they had more work to do than they could get through and wanted some one to help them. They sold the pupil's work as their own, just as people do now who take apprentices. When people can sell a pupil's work, they will teach the pupil all they know and will see he learns it. This is the secret of the whole matter.

The modern schoolmaster does not aim at learning from his pupils, he hardly can, but the old masters did. See how Giovanni Bellini learned from Titian and Giorgione who both came to him in the same year, as boys, when Bellini was 63 years old. What a day for painting was that! All Bellini's best work was done thenceforward. I know nothing in the history of art so touching as this. [1883.]

P. S. I have changed my mind about Titian. I don't like him. [1897.]

SAMUEL BUTLER
Note-Books (1912)

The subject would seem to be allegorical, but no satisfactory interpretation has yet been offered: the figures are tentatively identified as Orpheus, Circe with her wand, and Pan tempting Luna with white wool. The apprentice system described by Samuel Butler is well illustrated by the difficulty of attributing this particular painting. Generally ascribed to Bellini, it has also been given to Giorgione, to Titian, to Basaiti, and to some unidentified follower of Bellini, possibly Giulio Campagnola. Collections: Bardini, Paris. *Widener Collection,* 1942. Canvas. Height 18⅝ in.; width 32 in. (0.395 x 0.81). Painted c. 1515.

LORENZO LOTTO · Venetian c. 1480-1556

A Maiden's Dream

Already in the fifteenth century artists began to feel that landscape had become too tame and domesticated, and they set about exploring the mysterious and the unsubdued. These artists came from and worked for an urban population which had long since learnt to control natural forces. They therefore could view the old menaces of flood and forest with a kind of detachment. They could use them consciously to excite a pleasing horror. To this extent they may justifiably be called romantic. But it would be a mistake to suppose that they were similar to the Gothic novelists or the men of 1830. Horace Walpole wrote from the absolute security of Twickenham; to Grünewald, Altdorfer and Bosch the menaces of life were still real. . . . They knew that the human mind was full of darkness, twisted and fiery, and they painted an aspect of nature which expressed these dark convolutions of the spirit, just as the backgrounds of Piero della Francesca had expressed the clarity of the intellect. In doing so they no doubt made a conscious use of certain disturbing shapes and symbols. They are what we now call 'expressionist' artists, a term which is not as worthless as it sounds, because, in fact, the symbols of expressionism are remarkably consistent, and we find in the work of these early sixteenth-century landscape painters not only the same spirit but the same shapes and iconographical motives which recur in the work of such recent expressionists as van Gogh, Max Ernst, Graham Sutherland and Walt Disney. . . .

There is no doubt that Lotto was directly in touch with German painters. In his earliest painting, the *Maiden's Dream* in the National Gallery, Washington, which dates from about 1498, the trees and their relation to the distant landscape show unmistakably the influence of Dürer, who was in Venice in 1494-95, and foreshadow the forest landscapes which, in the next five years were to excite the imaginations of Altdorfer and Cranach. The *St. Jerome* in the Louvre, dated 1500, contains rocks and trees remarkably similar to the drawings which Dürer did on his journey home from Italy in 1495.

KENNETH CLARK
Landscape into Art (1949)

The resemblance between figures in Lotto's early altarpieces and the Saint Sebastian painted by Grünewald for the altar at Isenheim is further evidence of the connection between Lotto and German art, as Sir Kenneth Clark points out. Also the fact that Lotto painted portraits of Martin Luther and his wife suggests that he may have been in touch with the leaders of the Protestant Reformation. The subject of the painting reproduced has been considered by many critics to be a free interpretation of the Danaë myth. It seems more likely, however, to be Plutus dropping a shower of gold (in the semblance of flowers) upon the nymph Rhodos. Collections: Lord Conway, Maidstone, England. *Samuel H. Kress Collection*, 1939. Wood. Height 16⅞ in.; width 13¼ in. (0.43 x 0.34). Painted c. 1498.

GIORGIONE AND TITIAN · Venetian c. 1478-1510 AND c. 1477-1576

Portrait of a Venetian Gentleman

Giorgione forged the link between his teacher Giovanni Bellini and his illustrious pupil Titian. More significant however than his acknowledged historical achievement in connecting two epochs of expert painting is the truth that he remained independent of both. It was his destiny to make a unique aesthetic contribution. He invented the painted lyric. As in the more abstract art of music the meaning reaches us subtly, through the senses, and the subject is almost inseparable from the picture form. Such a conception of art was far from general acceptance even in Giorgione's enlightened day. . . . The broken parapet of the portrait. . . . has functional purpose in the pattern. Its reflecting surfaces and its angles are repeated in the open window thru which one can look across the Grand Canal to Palaces opposite and to a distant bridge. Amusingly its curve seems to repeat in its arch of light over dark water the prominent arched eyeball of the dark man portrayed. His expression is baffling — perhaps because he himself is baffled. We would like to know what troubles him. In his abstracted gaze we seem to see his determination to be resolute about something which is not yet satisfactorily settled in his own mind. His unseeing stare relates to the clenched fist on the closed book and perhaps even to the distant bridge at the Rialto. Thus a compact functioning of the lines is also contributory in every detail to the portrait's purpose of characterizing more than a man, of standing for a state of mind which the artist has known in himself and as a universally difficult moment of dangerous doubt and abrupt need for decision.

Duncan Phillips
The Leadership of Giorgione (1937)

This picture appears to date from a period when Titian and Giorgione were closely associated and frequently working in collaboration. Burroughs (*Art Criticism from a Laboratory*, 1938) has stated that the x-ray evidence indicates that the underpainting of the head resembles Giorgione's manner. The x-ray also shows that the hand originally grasped a sword, the hilt cutting across the space now occupied by the book; then the sword was repainted as a scroll; and finally, as a handkerchief. Possibly this painting is to be identified with "*A Man with a Sword*, by Giorgione" listed as at Somerset House in the inventory made of the Collection of King Charles I of England at the time of the sale of this collection (1649-1653). Collections: Henry Doetsch, London; Colonel George Kemp, Lord Rochdale, Beechwood Hall, England; Henry Goldman, New York. *Samuel H. Kress Collection,* 1939. Canvas. Height 30 in.; width 25 in. (0.76 x 0.64). Painted c. 1510.

TITIAN · VENETIAN c. 1477-1576

Venus with a Mirror

Tomorrow let loveless, let lover tomorrow make love:
O spring, singing spring, spring of the world renew!
In spring lovers consent and the birds marry
When the grove receives in her hair the nuptial dew.

    Tomorrow may loveless, may lover tomorrow make love.

Tomorrow's the day when the prime Zeus made love:
Out of lightning foam shot deep in the heaving sea
(Witnessed by green crowds of finny horses)
Dione rising and falling, he made to be!

    Tomorrow may loveless, may lover tomorrow make love.

Bidden unarmed to go and to go naked
Lest he destroy with bow, with dart, with brand—
Yet, girls, Cupid is pretty, and you must know
That Love unarmed can pierce with naked hand!

    Tomorrow may loveless, may lover tomorrow make love.

Over sky and land and down under the sea
On the path of the seed the goddess brought to earth
And dropped into our veins created fire,
That men might know the mysteries of birth.

    Tomorrow may loveless, may lover tomorrow make love.

ANONYMOUS
Pervigilium Veneris (3rd or 4th Century after Christ)

For Latin text see page 183. More than any other Renaissance artist Titian evokes the spirit of the ancient world. From his earliest masterpieces like the Bacchanals painted for the Duke of Ferrara to such late paintings as the picture reproduced, he repeatedly celebrated the power of Venus. These canvases are permeated with the same refined sensuality as that embodied in the poem *Pervigilium Veneris,* quoted above. Early records, together with many extant variations of the theme by Titian's studio and his later imitators and admirers, indicate that he painted at least three versions of the goddess of love gazing into a mirror. Only the present canvas is unanimously accepted as one of these three originals. It was bought in 1579 from Titian's son Pomponio by the Barbarigo family, Venice (in whose possession Ridolfi lists it in the seventeenth century), and passed from a branch of this family, about the middle of the last century, to the Hermitage Gallery, Leningrad. Collections: As above. *Mellon Collection*, 1937. Canvas. Height 49 in.; width 41½ in. (1.245 x 1.055). Painted c. 1555.

BOLTRAFFIO · Milanese 1467-1516

Portrait of a Youth

He was destined to learn his own wisdom apart from others or to learn the wisdom of others himself wandering among the snares of the world. The snares of the world were its ways of sin. He would fall. He had not yet fallen but he would fall silently, in an instant. Not to fall was too hard, too hard: and he felt the silent lapse of his soul, as it would be at some instant to come, falling, falling, but not yet fallen, still unfallen, but about to fall. . . . He drew forth a phrase from his treasure and spoke it softly to himself:

—A day of dappled seaborne clouds.—

. . . . Where was his boyhood now? Where was the soul that had hung back from her destiny, to brood alone upon the shame of her wounds and in her house of squalor and subterfuge to queen it in faded cerements and in wreaths that withered at the touch? Or, where was he. He was alone. He was unheeded, happy, and near to the wild heart of life. He was alone and young and wilful and wildhearted, alone amid a waste of wild air and brackish waters and the seaharvest of shells and tangle and veiled grey sunlight and gayclad lightclad figures of children and girls and voices childish and girlish in the air.

James Joyce
A Portrait of the Artist as a Young Man (1916)

Whoever is delighted with his own picture must derive his pleasure from the pleasure of another. Every man is always present to himself, and has, therefore, little need of his own resemblance, nor can desire it, but for the sake of those whom he loves, and by whom he hopes to be remembered. This use of the art is a natural and reasonable consequence of affection; and though, like other human actions, it is often complicated with pride, yet even such pride is more laudable than that by which palaces are covered with pictures, that, however excellent, neither imply the owner's virtue, nor excite it.

Samuel Johnson
The Idler (Feb. 24, 1759)

The portrait has sometimes been thought to be of the poet Girolamo Casio; but when Casio was the age of this boy, about twelve, the artist was only nine. The identity of the sitter will probably remain a mystery, but there is a curious clue. He apparently has lost one arm, for the artist is at some pains to show his empty right sleeve. Was this loss suffered in some heroic act of which his parents wished to be reminded? Was the prominence given to this mutilation "a natural and reasonable consequence of affection"? Perhaps in a forgotten archive in Lombardy lies buried the explanation of this strange effigy, so far as we know the unique representation in the Renaissance of a child with only one arm. The haunting quality of this painting, however, does not arise from an empty sleeve, touching as is this note of verisimilitude, but rather from the portrayal of that moment of transition between boyhood and adolescence which Joyce so sensitively describes. Collections: Baron Gustave de Rothschild, Paris; Sir Philip Sassoon, London. *Ralph and Mary Booth Collection*, 1947. Wood. Height 18½ in.; width 13¾ in. (0.47 x 0.35). Painted shortly before 1500.

BERNARDINO LUINI · Milanese c. 1480-1532

Portrait of a Lady

With education, the individuality of women in the upper classes was developed in the same way as that of men. Till the time of the Reformation, the personality of women out of Italy, even of the highest rank, comes forward but little. Exceptions like Isabella of Bavaria, Margaret of Anjou, and Isabella of Castille, are the forced result of very unusual circumstances. In Italy, throughout the whole of the fifteenth century, the wives of the rulers, and still more those of the Condottieri, have nearly all a distinct, recognizable personality, and take their share of notoriety and glory. To these came gradually to be added a crowd of famous women of the most varied kind; among them those whose distinction consisted in the fact that their beauty, disposition, education, virtue, and piety, combined to render them harmonious human beings. There was no question of 'woman's rights' or female emancipation, simply because the thing itself was a matter of course. The educated woman, no less than the man, strove naturally after a characteristic and complete individuality. The same intellectual and emotional development which perfected the man, was demanded for the perfection of the woman. Active literary work, nevertheless, was not expected from her, and if she were a poet, some powerful utterance of feeling, rather than the confidences of the novel or the diary, was looked for. These women had no thought of the public; their function was to influence distinguished men, and to moderate male impulse and caprice. . . .

Women of this stamp could listen to novels like those of Bandello, without social intercourse suffering from it. The ruling genius of society was not, as now, womanhood, or the respect for certain presuppositions, mysteries, and susceptibilities, but the consciousness of energy, of beauty, and of a social state full of danger and opportunity. And for this reason we find, side by side with the most measured and polished social forms, something our age would call immodesty, forgetting that by which it was corrected and counterbalanced — the powerful characters of the women who were exposed to it.

Jakob Burckhardt
Die Cultur der Renaissance in Italien (1860)

In order to paint a beautiful woman, I should need to see many of them, and have your Lordship's assistance in selecting the fairest. But since there is a dearth both of good judges and of beautiful women, I make use of a certain ideal that is in my mind. Whether it possesses any artistic excellence I do not know; but I try hard to see that it does.

Raphael
Letter to Baldassare Castiglione (1514)

There are few portraits by Luini and the present one is the most important of those on panel. In the light and shadow and in the smile, it shows the influence of Leonardo da Vinci, to whom some of Luini's works were formerly attributed. All the character and individuality that Burckhardt describes in the women of the period are here displayed with exceptional skill. For other ideals of feminine beauty see pages 141 and 147. Collections: Frederick Richards Leyland, London; Charles Fairfax Murray, Florence; Benson, London. *Mellon Collection*, 1937. Wood. Height 30⅜ in.; width 22⅝ in. (0.772 x 0.575). Painted c. 1515.

GIOVANNI BATTISTA MORONI · Brescian c. 1520-1578

"Titian's Schoolmaster"

The Master said, A gentleman takes as much trouble to discover what is right as lesser men take to discover what will pay.

The Master said, When natural substance prevails over ornamentation, you get the boorishness of the rustic. When ornamentation prevails over natural substance, you get the pedantry of the scribe. Only when ornament and substance are duly blended do you get the true gentleman.

'A gentleman can be broken, but cannot be dented; may be deceived, but cannot be led astray.'

The Master said, A true gentleman is calm and at ease; the Small Man is fretful and ill at ease.

The Master said, The gentleman calls attention to the good points in others; he does not call attention to their defects. The small man does just the reverse of this.

The Master said, 'The demands that a gentleman makes are upon himself; those that a small man makes are upon others.'

Master K'ung said, There are three things that a gentleman fears: he fears the will of Heaven, he fears great men, he fears the words of the Divine Sages. The small man does not know the will of Heaven and so does not fear it. He treats great men with contempt, and scoffs at the words of the Divine Sages.

Confucius
The Analects (6th or 5th Century b.c.)

Portraiture may be great art. There is a sense, indeed, in which it is perhaps the greatest art of any. And portraiture involves expression. Quite true, but expression of what? Of a passion, an emotion, a mood? Certainly not. Paint a man or woman with the damned 'pleasing expression,' or even the 'charmingly spontaneous' so dear to the 'photographic artist,' and you see at once that the thing is a mask, as silly as the old tragic and comic mask. The only expression allowable in great portraiture is the expression of character and moral quality, not of anything temporary, fleeting, accidental. Apart from portraiture you don't want even so much, or very seldom: in fact you only want types, symbols, suggestions. The moment you give what people call expression, you destroy the typical character of heads and degrade them into portraits which stand for nothing.

Edward Burne-Jones
Quoted, Georgiana Burne-Jones, *Memorials of Edward Burne-Jones* (1904)

Moroni has given his sitter that "expression of character and moral quality" which Burne-Jones emphasizes. The portrait epitomizes the Renaissance ideal of a gentleman, which found classic expression in Castiglione's *Il Cortegiano* (1528), and which is an ideal of some universality as Confucius bears witness. Hazlitt (*Sketches of the Principal Picture-Galleries in England,* 1824) said of the picture reproduced: "Not knowing any thing of Moroni, if we had been asked who had done it, we should have replied, '*Either Titian or the Devil.*'...but the eye in *Titian's School-master* is *an eye to look at, not to look with,* or if it looks *at* you, it does not look *through* you, which may be almost made a test of Titian's heads." The portrait was sketched by Van Dyck and copied by Rubens. For other views on portraiture, see pages 32, 40, 52, 90 and 96. Collections: Palazzo Borghese, Rome; Duke of Bridgewater, Bridgewater House, London; his nephew, 2nd Marquis of Stafford, Stafford House, London; his son, 2nd Duke of Sutherland, Stafford House, in which collection it remained until it came to America. *Widener Collection,* 1942. Canvas. Height 38⅛ in.; width 29¼ in. (0.97 x 0.74). Painted c. 1575.

PAOLO VERONESE · Venetian 1528-1588

The Finding of Moses

The historical and outwardly significant subjects of painting have often the disadvantage that just what is significant in them cannot be portrayed visually, but must be arrived at by thought. In this respect the *nominal* significance of the picture must be distinguished from its *real* significance. The former is the outward significance, which, however, occurs only as an additional conception; the latter is that side of the Idea of humanity which is made visible to the onlooker through the medium of the picture. For example, Moses found by the Egyptian princess is the nominal significance of a painting; it represents a moment of the greatest importance in history; the real significance, on the other hand, that which is really presented to the onlooker, is a foundling child rescued from its floating cradle by a noblewoman, an incident which may have happened often. It is the costume alone which enables the scholar to recognize the particular historical case; but the costume is of importance to the nominal significance only, while it is a matter of indifference to the real significance; to the latter only the human being as such, not the arbitrary forms, are of relevance. Subjects taken from history have no advantage over those which are taken from mere possibility, and which are therefore to be called, not individual, but merely general. For what is peculiarly significant in the former is not the individual, not the particular event as such, but the universal element in it, the side of the Idea of humanity which expresses itself through it.

ARTHUR SCHOPENHAUER
Die Welt als Wille und Vorstellung (1819)

Schopenhauer's aesthetics is not far removed from the theories of the Church Fathers. Though they would have given more importance to the nominalistic significance of the historical scene, they would have agreed with Schopenhauer that its real significance is its universal idea. Veronese was more modern in his point of view. Subject to him was merely an excuse for the display of formal values, the decorative effect of rich brocades, the interlocked thrust and counter-thrust of moving, gesticulating bodies, the composition of figures in space with all the complexities of linear and aerial perspective. These were his real interests and he became so indifferent to what was appropriate to the content of his scenes that he fell into difficulty with the Inquisition and barely escaped jail. Collections: Crozat (?), Paris; Louis-Michel Van Loo, Paris; Hermitage Gallery, Leningrad. *Mellon Collection*, 1937. Canvas. Height 22¾ in.; width 17½ in. (0.58 x 0.445). Probably painted in the early 1570's.

ALESSANDRO MAGNASCO · Genoese 1667-1749

The Baptism of Christ

From now on, artists wished painting to dominate its subject-matter, instead of being overruled by it. They had seen intimations of this attitude in the painters whom Manet recognized as men of his own kind: Delacroix, Hals and Goya. But it had never been deliberately or persistently adopted; in the work of previous artists it was accidental, restricted sometimes to a fragment or a single canvas, oftenest to a sketch. It showed itself whenever a painter fell to "drawing with his brush."

One has the impression that, like those Primitives who inserted their own faces alongside the donors', such artists wished to stamp their personality on the canvas—Rembrandt with the thick, broken arabesques of his sketches, Goya with his strong accents of pure black, Delacroix with his rageful slashes, and Hals, precursor of modern art, with his figures' strongly stylized hands. The provocative script of each was like a signature. And those who "signed" their work thus were the painters more interested in their medium than in what was being depicted. Yet, even so, script and medium remained at the service of portrayal. In Titian's last works, in Tintoretto, the accented brush-strokes subserve dramatic lyricism; in Rembrandt also, though his lyricism lies deep below the surface. Not without qualms did Delacroix give play to those fierce slashes, like Rubens at his stormiest. Sometimes Goya goes farthest of them all; but Goya (if we disregard his setting and his fierce antipathies) *is* modern art.

Then there was one of Guardi's manners, and one of Magnasco's. Where we have Magnasco at his best, the frenzied line, all in notes of exclamation, seems to follow the play of a light that frets the contours of objects and figures—that "frill of light" which Ingres thought beneath the dignity of art. This light is ever with him; even when he does not body it forth, the brush-strokes follow its unseen ripples. But, amazing as was the achievement of that dazzling Italian tragicomedy, it had quite definite limits.

ANDRÉ MALRAUX
Psychologie de l'art (1947)

"The frenzied line" which Malraux mentions made Magnasco's work a subject of controversy in the eighteenth century. As his biographer, Carlo Giuseppe Ratti, wrote in 1769: "Magnasco's staccato brushwork seemed to be of no account, even ridiculous, to certain people, who thought all the beauty of painting consisted in a smooth appearance or in a servile imitation of the least minutiae, to which a lively, vivacious spirit is incapable of submitting. And yet Magnasco was a painter of such poetic inspiration and fantasy that he was surpassed by no one else amongst us and far outstripped many. His style with its short swift strokes should have gained credit for him rather than disesteem; but he found himself in a city where there was no genuine appreciation of this new manner." Collections: Sambon, Paris; Geiger, Venice. *Samuel H. Kress Collection,* 1939. Canvas. Height 46¼ in.; width 57¾ in (1.17 x 1.47). Painted between 1735 and 1749, in the artist's Genoese period.

PIETRO LONGHI · Venetian 1702-1785

Blind Man's Buff

In Pietro Longhi Venice developed a sympathetic chronicler of her social pleasures. The world of his delicate and witty little canvases is that of the card party, the formal call, the vanity and ceremony of philandering, the shop, the musicale, the masked ball. Only Holland has given so true and sympathetic a record of her smaller affairs, and at the moment, only Hogarth in England and Chardin in France were doing the thing with equal ability.

Nothing better shows the slightly anachronistic quality of Tiepolo's grandeur than a fine Longhi. The Venetian imagination had moved indoors, so to speak, had foregone in favor of individual gratifications the old vision of the collective splendor. Venice no longer dines grandly in the open with Veronese, she coquettishly sips coffee with Longhi. If she had declined in nobility, she had at least kept her sincerity and taste. Her affair had ever been rather with appearances than with ideals or interpretations. But since the Greeks no other nation had considered appearances with such noble candor. She kept to the end the good pictorial habit of letting appearances explain themselves. Thus if a Titian will stand beside a Pheidian marble, so will a Tiepolo beside an Alexandrian masterpiece, while a trim belle of Pietro Longhi need feel no confusion before a Tanagra figurine. Time passes gently over a city whose artistic aims are as limited as her taste is sure. Venice had ever been gracious in her grandeur, and gracious she remained even after she had ceased to be grand.

FRANK JEWETT MATHER, JR.
A History of Italian Painting (1923)

The world inhabited by Longhi's figures seems too large for them. They look like prematurely old children dressed for a masquerade. If the people playing Blind Man's Buff were to seat themselves at their buffet, only their heads would be visible above the table top. At least twelve feet of damask seems to rise above these Lilliputians, and yet one feels this is less than half the height of the room. Amid the great buildings of Venice the citizens of the Republic, as depicted by Longhi, seem to have shrunk, just as their power and authority have dwindled away. Their minuscule frivolity betokens the decline of their city from a seat of Empire to a pleasure resort of Europe (see page 76). Collections: Giovanelli Collection, Venice. *Samuel H. Kress Collection,* 1939. Canvas. Height 19¼ in.; width 24 in. (0.49 x 0.61). Painted c. 1760.

GIOVANNI PAOLO PANINI · Roman 1691/92-1765

The Interior of the Pantheon

But the grace of this market, and indeed the admiration of the whole world, is the Pantheon, now called S. Maria della Rotonda, formerly sacred to all the Gods, and still remaining the most entire antiquity of the city. It was built by Marcus Agrippa, as testifies the architrave of the portico, sustained by thirteen pillars of Theban marble, six feet thick, and fifty-three in height, of one entire stone. In this porch is an old inscription.

Entering the church, we admire the fabric, wholly covered with one cupola, seemingly suspended in the air, and receiving light by a hole in the middle only. The structure is near as high as broad, viz. 144 feet, not counting the thickness of the walls, which is twenty-two more to the top, all of white marble, and till Urban VIII. converted part of the metal into ordnance of war against the Duke of Parma, and part to make the high altar in St. Peter's, it was all over covered with Corinthian brass, ascending by forty degrees within the roof, or convex, of the cupola, richly carved with octagons in the stone. There are niches in the walls, in which stood heretofore the statues of Jupiter and the other Gods and Goddesses; for here was that Venus which had hung in her ear the other Union that Cleopatra was about to dissolve and drink up, as she had done its fellow. There are several of these niches, one above another, for the celestial, terrestrial, and subterranean deities; but the place is now converted into a church dedicated to the Blessed Virgin and all the Saints. The pavement is excellent, and the vast folding-gates, of Corinthian brass. In a word, it is of all the Roman antiquities the most worthy of notice.

JOHN EVELYN
Diary (Feb. 21, 1645)

The painting of architectural monuments flourished in the eighteenth century. This was the period of the Grand Tour, which began earlier with travelers like John Evelyn. Views of cities and buildings were collected by such tourists on a large scale. However, few if any of the architectural painters reached the level achieved by the present picture, and Panini himself rarely revealed the qualities shown here. Collections: *Samuel H. Kress Collection,* 1939. Canvas. Height 50½ in.; width 39 in. (1.28 x 0.99). Painted c. 1740.

FRANCESCO GUARDI · Venetian 1712-1793

View on the Cannaregio, Venice

In Venice Tasso's echoes are no more,
And silent rows the songless gondolier;
Her palaces are crumbling to the shore,
And music meets not always now the ear:
Those days are gone — but Beauty still is here.
States fall, arts fade — but Nature doth not die,
Nor yet forget how Venice once was dear,
The pleasant place of all festivity,
The revel of the earth, the masque of Italy! . . .

I loved her from my boyhood; she to me
Was as a fairy city of the heart,
Rising like water-columns from the sea,
Of joy the sojourn, and of wealth the mart;
And Otway, Radcliffe, Schiller, Shakspeare's art,
Had stamp'd her image in me, and even so,
Although I found her thus, we did not part;
Perchance even dearer in her day of woe,
Than when she was a boast, a marvel, and a show.

GEORGE GORDON, LORD BYRON
Childe Harold's Pilgrimage (1818)

There can be nothing more poetical in its aspect than the city of Venice; does this depend upon the sea, or the canals? —

"The dirt and sea-weed whence proud Venice rose?"

Is it the canal which runs between the palace and the prison, or the "Bridge of Sighs," which connects them, that render it poetical? Is it the "Canal Grande," or Rialto which arches it, the churches which tower over it, the palaces which line, and the gondolas which glide over the waters, that render this city more poetical than Rome itself? Mr. B. will say, perhaps, that the Rialto is but marble, the palaces and churches only stone, and the gondolas a "coarse" black cloth, thrown over some planks of carved wood, with a shining bit of fantastically formed iron at the prow, *"without"* the water. And I tell him that without these, the water would be nothing but a clay-coloured ditch; and whoever says the contrary, deserves to be at the bottom of that, where Pope's heroes are embraced by the mud nymphs. There would be nothing to make the Canal of Venice more poetical than that of Paddington, were it not for the artificial adjuncts above mentioned, although it is a perfectly natural canal, formed by the sea, and the innumerable islands which constitute the site of this extraordinary city.

GEORGE GORDON, LORD BYRON
Letter to John Murray (Feb. 7, 1821)

Collections: Chiesa Collection, Milan. *Samuel H. Kress Collection,* 1939. Canvas. Height 18¾ in.; width 29¼ in. (0.48 x 0.74). Painted c. 1770.

EL GRECO · SPANISH 1541-1614

Saint Martin and the Beggar

Toledo is a knife. Greco has cut his name deeply into its blade. . . .

Hidden rhythm is developed from one end to the other of Greco's canvases.

Never mind about those square clouds, or that flat face, or that enormous leg. Nature must obey, and allow herself to be used to fill such spaces as this imperious master may assign to her.

Whether it is Greco or Cézanne, these skilful groupings and camouflaged problems on which the picture's harmony depends — these basement kitchens as it were — may be mistaken for either childishness or madness.

Barrès, though not so blind as to fall into that error, accounts for the deformations in Greco's pictures on sentimental grounds. He will only admit a spasm — the spiritualization of the body — instead of seeing that it is also largely a question of architecture. 'Architecture corrected by emotion.'

Greco is first and foremost a painter, and should not be confounded with the intellectual Leonardo.

JEAN COCTEAU
Visites à Maurice Barrès (1924)

There is no Excellent *Beauty*, that hath not some Strangenesse in the Proportion.

FRANCIS BACON
Essayes (1625)

Painted for the Chapel of San José, Toledo, this painting is documented by the original contract, dated November 20, 1597, which states that El Greco is to be paid 31,328 reales. This was an unusually high price and it was necessary for El Greco to sue for payment. The fact that Saint Martin, when represented as a soldier, rides a white horse is explained by G. G. King (*Art Bulletin*, 1922), as a reference to the vision in Revelation, vi, 2, in which the rider on a white horse "went forth conquering, and to conquer." Saint Martin dividing his cloak with a beggar was a favorite subject in Spain, and especially with El Greco. The present painting is probably the first of his several versions that have been preserved. Collections: Chapel of San José, Toledo. *Widener Collection*, 1942. Canvas. Height 76⅛ in.; width 40½ in. (1.935 x 1.03). Painted 1597-99.

EL GRECO · SPANISH 1541-1614

Laocoön

A greater omen and of worse portent
Did our unwary minds with fear torment,
Concurring to produce the dire event.
Laocoön, Neptune's priest by lot that year,
With solemn pomp then sacrificed a steer,
When, dreadful to behold, from sea we spied
Two serpents, ranked abreast, the seas divide,
And smoothly sweep along the swelling tide.
Their flaming crests above the waves they show;
Their bellies seem to burn the seas below;
Their speckled tails advance to steer their course,
And on the sounding shore the flying billows force.
And now the strand, and now the plain they held,
Their ardent eyes with bloody streaks were filled;
Their nimble tongues they brandished as they came,
And licked their hissing jaws, that spluttered flame.
We fled amazed. Their destined way they take,
And to Laocoön and his children make.
And first around the tender boys they wind,
Then with their sharpened fangs their limbs and bodies grind.
The wretched father, running to their aid
With pious haste, but vain, they next invade.
Twice round his waist their winding volumes rolled,
And twice about his gasping throat they fold.
The priest thus doubly choked, their crests divide,
And towering o'er his head, in triumph ride.
With both his hands he labours at the knots,
His holy fillets the blue venom blots;
His roaring fills the flitting air around.
Thus, when an ox receives a glancing wound,
He breaks his bands, the fatal halter flies,
And with loud bellowings breaks the yielding skies.
Their tasks performed, the serpents quit their prey,
And to the tower of Pallas made their way.
Couched at her feet, they lie protected there
By her large buckler and protended spear.

VIRGIL
Aeneid (c. 19 B.C.)

For Latin text see page 183. Although El Greco was born a Greek, he painted only one subject derived from the history or mythology of Greece, the story of Laocoön and his sons. Possibly it was the sculptured group of the Laocoön, discovered in 1506 and exhibited in the Vatican during El Greco's sojourn in Rome, that inspired him to paint his interpretation of the legend. Among the several versions of the story in Greek and Latin, Virgil's is the most famous; it is uncertain which version El Greco followed. The two figures at the right have been conjectured to be Apollo and Diana; but if El Greco was following Virgil, it is possible the male figure is Aeneas, the narrator, and the female, Dido, to whom the story is told. In the background is a view of El Greco's adopted home, Toledo. Collections: Probably the large painting of Laocoön listed in 1614 in the inventory of El Greco's estate in Toledo; Dukes of Montpensier, Seville; Palace of San Telmo, Seville; Infante Don Antonio de Orleans, Sanlúcar de Barrameda; E. Fischer, Charlottenburg; Prince Paul of Yugoslavia, Belgrade. *Samuel H. Kress Collection,* 1939. Canvas. Height 54⅛ in.; width 68 in. (1.375 x 1.725). Painted c. 1610.

VELAZQUEZ · Spanish 1599-1660

The Needlewoman

Now, in the usual "pictures of the year" there is but one flesh, that shall do service under all circumstances, whether the person painted be in the soft light of the room or out in the glare of the open. The one aim of the unsuspecting painter is to make his man "stand out" from the frame—never doubting that, on the contrary, he should really, and in truth absolutely does, stand *within* the frame—and at a depth behind it equal to the distance at which the painter sees his model. The frame is, indeed, the window through which the painter looks at his model, and nothing could be more offensively inartistic than this brutal attempt to thrust the model on the hitherside of this window!

Yet this is the false condition of things to which all have become accustomed, and in the stupendous effort to bring it about, exaggeration has been exhausted—and the traditional means of the incompetent can no further go.

Lights have been heightened until the white of the tube alone remains—shadows have been deepened until black alone is left. Scarcely a feature stays in its place, so fierce is its intention of "firmly" coming forth; and in the midst of this unseemly struggle for prominence, the gentle truth has but a sorry chance, falling flat and flavourless, and without force.

The Master from Madrid, himself, beside this monster success of mediocrity, would be looked upon as mild: *beau bien sure, mais pas "dans le mouvement"!*

Whereas, could the people be induced to turn their eyes but for a moment, with the fresh power of comparison, upon their fellow-creatures as they pass in the gallery, they might be made dimly to perceive (though I doubt it, so blind is their belief in the bad) how little they resemble the impudent images on the walls!... And then it might be explained to their riveted intelligence how they had mistaken meretriciousness for mastery, and by what mean methods the imposture had been practised upon them.

JAMES A. MCNEILL WHISTLER
The Gentle Art of Making Enemies (1890)

Whistler learned from "the Master from Madrid," as he called Velázquez, to paint in a restricted key. This is a practice that Alberti also stresses (see page 16). Such organization of tone was often ignored by fashionable painters like Sargent and Boldini, who frequently exaggerated high lights and illusionistic feats of modeling until their sitters often seem to step out of the frame. The painting reproduced, thought to be of Velázquez's daughter and probably identical with the "Head of a Woman Sewing" recorded in the inventory of his studio at the time of his death, is a good illustration of the principles Whistler was preaching. Collections: Marquis de Keriaval, Brittany; Mme. Christiane de Polès, Paris. *Mellon Collection,* 1937. Canvas. Height 29 in.; width 23⅝ in. (0.737 x 0.60). Painted c. 1640.

MURILLO · Spanish 1617-1682

The Return of the Prodigal Son

If there be a real law of Nature, that is to say any instinct that is universally and permanently rooted in animals and men (which is not beyond dispute), I may say that, in my opinion, next to the anxiety for self-preservation and avoiding what is harmful, which is possessed by every animal, the affection which the begetter has for his offspring takes the second place. And, because Nature seems to have recommended to us this affection, looking to the extension and advance of the successive parts of this her machine, it is not to be wondered at if the love of children towards their parents, since it goes backwards, is not so great.

To which may be added that other Aristotelian consideration, that the man who benefits another loves him better than he is loved by the other; and that he to whom a thing is owing loves better than he who owes. Every artisan loves his work better than he would be loved by the work if it had feeling; since Being is a thing to be cherished, and Being consists in motion and action. Wherefore every one in some sort lives in his work. He who benefits another does a beautiful and worthy deed; he who receives, only a useful one. Now the useful is much less to be loved than the beautiful. The beautiful is stable and permanent, affording him who has exercised it a constant gratification. The useful is easily lost and escapes, nor is the memory of it either so fresh or so pleasing. Those things are most dear to us that have cost us most; and it is more difficult to give than to take.

Michel de Montaigne
Essais (1595)

The French military commander, Marshal Soult, carried back from the conquest of Spain hundreds of paintings which are now scattered over Europe. Among those looted pictures, which were sold after the collapse of Napoleon, was The Prodigal Son. Originally it formed part of the decoration of the church built by the Brotherhood of La Caridad in Seville in connection with their Hospital of Saint George. The present canvas, together with Moses Striking the Rock (still in La Caridad), Abraham and the Angels (until lately in Stafford House and now in the National Gallery of Canada), and San Juan de Dios (La Caridad), hung on the Gospel side of the nave. On the opposite side its counterpart was Christ Healing the Paralytic (National Gallery, London), and the other compositions were the Miracle of the Loaves and Fishes (La Caridad), Saint Peter in Prison (Hermitage, Leningrad), and Saint Elizabeth of Hungary (Academy of San Fernando, Madrid). Collections: La Caridad, Seville; Marshal Soult, Paris; Duke of Sutherland, Stafford House, London. *Given by the Avalon Foundation through the generosity of Ailsa Mellon Bruce,* 1948. Canvas. Height 93 in.; width 102¾ in. (2.363 x 2.61). Painted between 1670 and 1674.

HANS MEMLING · Flemish 1430/35-1494

Madonna and Child with Angels

Fle we to our Lord and we shall be comforted; touch we him and we shall be made clene; cleve
to him and we shall be sekir and safe fro al maner of peril. For our curtes Lord will that we ben as
homley with him as herte may thinke or soule may desiren. But beware that we taken not so reklesly
this homleyhede that we levyn curtesy. For our Lord himselfe is sovereyn homleyhede, and as homley
as he is, as curtes he is, for he is very curtes. And the blissid creatures that shall ben in hevyn with him
without end, he will have them like to himselfe in all things. And to be like our Lord perfectly, it is
our very salvation and our full bliss. And if we wott not how we shall don all this, desire we of our
Lord and he shal lerne us. For it is his owne likeing and his worship; blissid mot he be.

The Lady Julian of Norwich
Revelations of Divine Love (1373)

It is easy to underrate or overrate Hans Memling. The greatness of his technical gift is obvious,
but so is the narrowness of his imagination. His attractiveness within his range has never needed and
never lacked celebration. As the culminating figure of late Gothic painting both in a material and
spiritual way he is highly important. A full generation before he was born the Van Eycks were trying
to give oil painting a splendor which the Northern world had earlier seen only in stained glass and
enamels. It remained for Memling to bring that splendor to a radiance beyond which no merely
coloristic progress was possible. On the spiritual side Memling made for the first time visible all those
tendernesses towards the Virgin and the virgin saints which the Middle Ages had expressed lyrically
in Latin and vernacular poetry. After Memling, everyone could see what had been the private,
chivalric ardor of a few mystics who were also poets. Others made the attempt, notably his immediate
predecessors of the Cologne school, but no one struck the note so lovingly and with such richness of
overtones. To have created an enduring symbolism for this exquisite phase of the beauty of holiness,
is surely distinction enough for any artist.

Frank Jewett Mather, Jr.
Western European Painting of the Renaissance (1939)

Glossary: *sekir*, secure; *curtes*, courteous;
homleyhede, homeliness, intimacy; *levyn*, leave.

Fromentin (*Les Maîtres d'autrefois*, 1876) also has described the peculiar charm of Memling's paintings, especially evident in the
picture reproduced. "Imagine, in the midst of the horrors of the century, a privileged spot, a sort of angelical retreat ideally silent
and enclosed, where passions are quieted and troubles cease, where people pray and adore, where everything is transfigured, physical ugliness and moral ugliness, where new feelings arise, where simplicity, gentleness, and supernatural mildness grow, like
lilies — and you will have an idea of the unique soul of Memling, and the miracle he works in his pictures." Collections:
Gotisches Haus, Wörlitz (Ducal Collection of Anhalt-Dessau), Germany. *Mellon Collection*, 1937. Wood. Height 23⅛ in.;
width 18⅞ in. (0.59 x 0.48). Painted c. 1480.

PETRUS CHRISTUS · Flemish c. 1410-1472/73

The Nativity

The mystic insight begins with the sense of a mystery unveiled, of a hidden wisdom now suddenly become certain beyond the possibility of a doubt. The sense of certainty and revelation comes earlier than any definite belief. . . .

The first and most direct outcome of the moment of illumination is belief in the possibility of a way of knowledge which may be called revelation or insight or intuition, as contrasted with sense, reason, and analysis, which are regarded as blind guides leading to the morass of illusion. Closely connected with this belief is the conception of a Reality behind the world of appearance and utterly different from it. This Reality is regarded with an admiration often amounting to worship; it is felt to be always and everywhere close at hand, thinly veiled by the shows of sense, ready, for the receptive mind, to shine in its glory even through the apparent folly and wickedness of Man. The poet, the artist, and the lover are seekers after that glory: the haunting beauty that they pursue is the faint reflection of its sun. But the mystic lives in the full light of the vision: what others dimly seek he knows, with a knowledge beside which all other knowledge is ignorance.

BERTRAND RUSSELL
Mysticism and Logic (1914)

That "mystic insight" Bertrand Russell describes is evident in the paintings of Petrus Christus, especially in the Nativity here reproduced. But this mood of illumination, this sense of a reality just behind the world of appearance is evoked by scenes of exceptional actuality. As Roger Fry has said (*Flemish Art,* 1927): "Not only was Christus able to construct credible volumes, he pushed even further than Hubert van Eyck the possibilities of situating them in a credible space. . . . we feel the space around each of the figures and we realize fully their relatively greater or less recession from the eye. Of course, in any picture which has verisimilitude we *know* which figure is meant to be in front of which — of course, when we see a tree drawn the size of a thumbnail beside a life-sized face we know it must be a long way back, but in most Flemish primitive pictures we only know this as it were by deduction, the space and the volumes are not clearly present to the imagination as they are here." Collections: Prince Manuel Yturbe, Madrid; Duchess of Parcent, Madrid. *Mellon Collection,* 1937. Wood. Height 51¼ in.; width 38¼ in. (1.30 x 0.97). Painted c. 1445-46, according to Tolnay (*Magazine of Art,* 1941); somewhat later, according to J. Held (*Art Bulletin,* 1942).

LUCAS CRANACH, THE ELDER · German 1472-1553

A Prince of Saxony

What gives to portraits their principal charm is simplicity. I do not count as portraits those pictures in which the artist seeks to idealize the features of a celebrated man whom he has not seen but whom he paints from traditional likenesses; invention has the right to enter into such representations. True portraits are those that one does from one's contemporaries: we like to see them on the canvas as we meet them around us, even in the case of illustrious persons.

Eugène Delacroix
Journal (July 29, 1854)

The production of a work of art throws a light upon the mystery of humanity. A work of art is an abstract or epitome of the world. It is the result or expression of nature, in miniature. For although the works of nature are innumerable and all different, the result or the expression of them all is similar and single. Nature is a sea of forms radically alike and even unique. A leaf, a sunbeam, a landscape, the ocean, make an analogous impression on the mind. What is common to them all, — that perfectness and harmony, is beauty. The standard of beauty is the entire circuit of natural forms, — the totality of nature; which the Italians expressed by defining beauty "il più nell' uno." Nothing is quite beautiful alone; nothing but is beautiful in the whole. A single object is only so far beautiful as it suggests this universal grace. The poet, the painter, the sculptor, the musician, the architect, seek each to concentrate this radiance of the world on one point, and each in his several work to satisfy the love of beauty which stimulates him to produce. Thus is Art a nature passed through the alembic of man. Thus in art does Nature work through the will of a man filled with the beauty of her first works.

Ralph Waldo Emerson
Nature (1883)

It has been suggested by Friedländer and Rosenberg (1932) that the sitter in this portrait may be Prince Frederick (born 1504), the son of Duke George the Bearded. For other views on portraiture, see pages 32, 40, 52, 66 and 96. Collections: A. Salomon, Dresden. *Ralph and Mary Booth Collection,* 1947. Wood. Height 17¼ in.; width 13⅜ in. (0.438 x 0.345). Painted c. 1517.

HANS HOLBEIN, THE YOUNGER · German 1497-1543

Sir Brian Tuke

Holbein, in fact, was a great Renderer. If I wanted to find a figure really akin to his I think I should go to music and speak of Bach. For in Bach you have just that peculiar Teutonic type of which Holbein is so great an example: in the musician too you have that marvellous mastery of the instrument, that composure, that want of striving. And both move one by what musicians call "absolute" means. . . .

We are, literally, in love with this arrangement of lines, of lights and of shadows. The eye is held by no object, but solely by the music of the pattern — the quality that we call "Holbein". . . .

Simplicity and severity were probably distasteful enough to him. Thus nothing could have been further from his sympathy than what is best in modern decorative art, and he had little or no idea, beyond that enforced by the exigencies of space, of adapting his design to the form of the object to be decorated or of reducing the amount of ornament further and further until the best decorated space be that which contains the least ornament. *His* dukes would never have been the worst dressed men of a House of Peers.

His is the other end of our line, in this as in so many other things, and to appreciate him thoroughly we have to make mental efforts of one kind and another. As we might put it, he was vulgar, which we are not, but he had more blood and more hope, so that he achieved the impossible so many times, and climbing in places where we are accustomed to say that climbing is wrong or hopeless, he appears on peaks more high than any of ours. That, of course, is what the master does in the realm of the arts.

Ford Madox Ford
Hans Holbein the Younger (1905)

"Holbein's heads are to the finest portraits what state-papers are to history," Hazlitt remarked. "We need hardly observe that they all have character in the extreme, so that we may be said to be acquainted with the people they represent; but then they give nothing but character, and only one part of that, *viz.* the dry, the literal, the concrete, and fixed. They want the addition of passion and beauty; but they are the finest *caput mortuums* of expression that ever were made. Hans Holbein had none of the volatile essence of genius in his composition. If portrait-painting is the prose of the art, his pictures are the prose of portrait-painting." Sir Brian Tuke was secretary to Henry VIII, in which capacity it was his business to pay Holbein's salary. He was also "governor of the king's post" and therefore to some degree responsible for founding the postal system in England. Collections: Philip Sidney, 3rd Earl of Leicester; Sir Paul Methuen, and descendants, among whom the last owner was Paul, 1st Lord Methuen, Corsham Court, Chippenham, Wiltshire; Richard Sanderson, Edinburgh; Richard, 2nd Marquess of Westminster; Lady Theodora Guest, Inwood, Templecombe, England; Watson B. Dickerman, New York. *Mellon Collection,* 1937. Wood. Height 19⅜ in.; width 15¼ in. (0.493 x 0.387). Painted 1526-28.

BRIANVS TVKE, MILES.   AN ETATIS SVÆ, LVII

. DROIT ET   AVANT.

NVNQVID NON PAVCITAS DIERVM
MEORVM FINIETVR BREVI ?

SIR ANTHONY VAN DYCK · FLEMISH 1599-1641

Marchesa Balbi

Oblivion is not to be hired: The greater part must be content to be as though they had not been, to be found in the register of God, not in the record of man. Twenty seven names make up the first story, and the recorded names ever since contain not one living Century. The number of the dead long exceedeth all that shall live. The night of time far surpasseth the day, and who knows when was the Æquinox? Every houre addes unto that current Arithmetique, which scarce stands one moment. And since death must be the Lucina of life, and even Pagans could doubt whether thus to live, were to die; Since our longest Sun sets at right descensions, and makes but winter arches, and therefore it cannot be long before we lie down in darknesse, and have our light in ashes; Since the brother of death daily haunts us with dying *memento's,* and time that grows old it self, bids us hope no long duration: Diuturnity is a dream and folly of expectation.

SIR THOMAS BROWNE
Hydriotaphia (1658)

Portraiture is an attempt to buy off oblivion, in some cases a successful attempt. Yet how much has been forgotten about sitters whose effigies nevertheless survive because fashioned by genius! An historian, Menotti (*L'Arte,* 1899), has tried to prove that the Marchesa Balbi, like Van Dyck, was born in Antwerp. If this is correct, was it she who introduced her young compatriot on his Italian journey to the patrician society of Genoa, whose portraits he painted with more inspiration than he was ever to show again? Was there some romantic attachment between these two aliens from the North? These are questions we shall never be able to answer; facts about the Marchesa's life are to be found only "in the register of God, not in the record of man." Collections: Balbi family, Genoa; Baron J. B. Heath, Genoa; Robert Stayner Holford, London; Sir George Lindsay Holford, London. *Mellon Collection,* 1937. Canvas. Height 72 in.; width 48 in. (1.83 x 1.22). Painted in Genoa between 1622 and 1627.

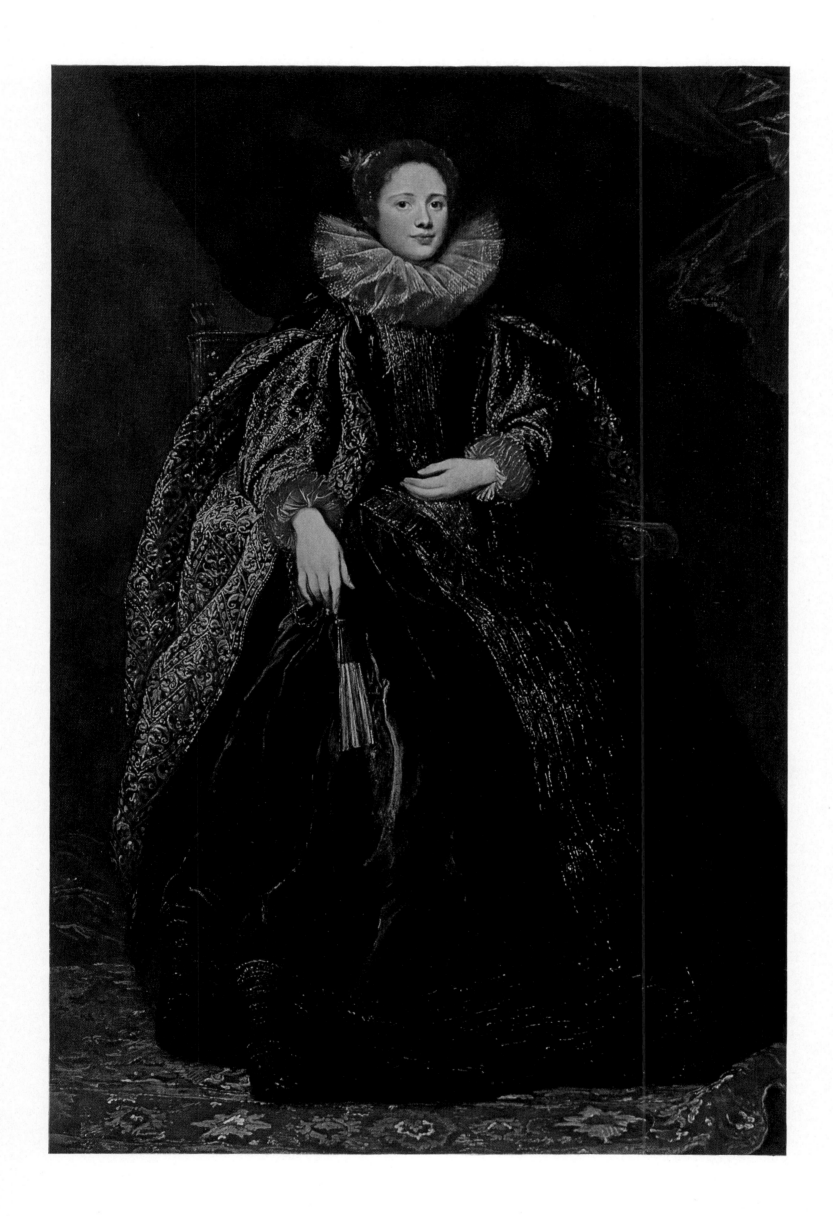

REMBRANDT · Dutch 1606-1669

A Polish Nobleman

More and more does his sympathy go out to the feelings of others. More and more the tenderness of the Bible story — the human side of it, its perpetual lessons — are embodied in every drama that he paints or draws, in the very portraits that he paints. The men and women, whoever they may be, the artisan, the theologian, the nobleman, the professional man, the plain people or the wealthy — are looked at each as having a history behind them. Something of an individual soul unlike any other individual spirit, with special experiences, shines within his portraits or imagined faces in a way that no one before or after him has attained, or even perhaps has dreamed of attaining. Each and all of these portraits are, as it were, historic. They are important even if we have no idea of what they represent; and indeed it is in those cases that this individuality of previous existence appeals to us most strongly. They are the nearest approach ever made to actual being, and perhaps exist more powerfully in the pictures than our unperceptive eyes could make out had we the real men and women before us. Before his great portraits the refined crowd gazing upon them in the galleries seems tamer and less valuable. They are the common people; and Rembrandt's paintings of any ordinary acquaintance are the elect and the wonderful. . . .

For after all, it is as the great dreamer that Rembrandt stands almost alone, unless we choose to think of him with such other dreamers as Michelangelo or Shakespeare. He remains the great exponent of the pity and tenderness of Bible story, of its being of all times, and a synopsis of all human life; and he remains, as well, the master of many realities, the poet of the mystery of light, and the painter of the individual human soul.

JOHN LA FARGE
Great Masters (1903)

La Farge is making Aristotle's point that the great portrait expresses the Universal rather than the particular (see supra, p. 32). Rembrandt, he points out, paints the typical and does not attempt to do a faithful portrait of an individual, however much of a likeness he may actually have achieved. From this point of view it is interesting that the nominalistic nineteenth century identified the painting as either John III Sobieski or Stephen Báthory, Kings of Poland, attempts at identification which have been discredited by later Rembrandt critics. For other views on portraiture, see pages 32, 40, 52, 66 and 90. Collections: The Hermitage Gallery, Leningrad. *Mellon Collection,* 1937. Wood. Height 38⅛ in.; width 26 in. (0.97 x 0.66). Signed, and dated 1637.

REMBRANDT · Dutch 1606-1669

Portrait of a Lady with an Ostrich-Feather Fan

What then did those immortals see, the writers who aimed at all which is greatest, and scorned the accuracy which lies in every detail? They saw many other things, and they also saw this, that Nature determined man to be no low or ignoble animal; but introducing us into life and this entire universe as into some vast assemblage, to be spectators, in a sort, of her entirety, and most ardent competitors, did then implant in our souls an invincible and eternal love of that which is great and, by our own standard, more divine. Therefore it is, that for the speculation and thought which are within the scope of human endeavour not all the universe together is sufficient, our conceptions often pass beyond the bounds which limit it; and if a man were to look upon life all round, and see how in all things the extraordinary, the great, the beautiful stand supreme, he will at once know for what ends we have been born. So it is that, as by some physical law, we admire, not surely the little streams, transparent though they be, and useful too, but Nile, or Tiber, or Rhine, and far more than all, Ocean; nor are we awed by this little flame of our kindling, because it keeps its light clear, more than by those heavenly bodies, often obscured though they be, nor think it more marvellous than the craters of Etna, whose eruptions bear up stones and entire masses, and sometimes pour forth rivers of that Titanic and unalloyed fire. Regarding all such things we may say this, that what is serviceable or perhaps necessary to man, man can procure; what passes his thought wins his wonder.

Hence, when we speak of men of great genius in literature, where the greatness does not necessarily fall outside the needs and service of man, we must at once arrive at the conclusion, that men of this stature, though far removed from flawless perfection, yet all rise above the mortal: other qualities prove those who possess them to be men, sublimity raises them almost to the intellectual greatness of God. No failure, no blame; but greatness has our very wonder. What need still to add, that each of these great men is often seen to redeem all his failures by a single sublimity, a single success; and further, which is most convincing, that if we were to pick out all the failures of Homer, Demosthenes, Plato, and the other greatest writers, and to mass them together, the result would be a small, an insignificant fraction of the successes which men of that heroic build exhibit everywhere. Therefore every age and all time, which envy itself can never prove to be in its dotage, has bestowed upon them the assured prizes of victory.

Longinus
On the Sublime (1st or 2nd Century after Christ)

In the Portrait of a Lady with an Ostrich-Feather Fan Rembrandt has touched the sublime. Here is an example of the Grand Style — that "perfection of expression in every direction and kind" — at its peak. There is a possibility that this picture and its pendant, the Portrait of a Gentleman with a Tall Hat and Gloves, also in the National Gallery of Art. represent the painter Ter Borch and his wife some ten years later than they are shown in Ter Borch's own paintings in the Rijksmuseum, Amsterdam. Collections: Prince Youssoupoff, Leningrad. *Widener Collection*, 1942. Canvas. Height 39¼ in.; width 32⅝ in. (0.995 x 0.83). Signed, and dated 166(7?).

REMBRANDT · DUTCH 1606-1669

The Descent from the Cross

Desire for nothing known in my maturer years,
When joy grew mad with awe, at counting future tears.
When, if my spirit's sky was full of flashes warm,
I knew not whence they came, from sun or thunder-storm.

But, first, a hush of peace — a soundless calm descends;
The struggle of distress, and fierce impatience ends;
Mute music soothes my breast — unuttered harmony,
That I could never dream, till Earth was lost to me.

Then dawns the Invisible; the Unseen its truth reveals;
My outward sense is gone, my inward essence feels:
Its wings are almost free — its home, its harbour found,
Measuring the gulf, it stoops — and dares the final bound.

Oh! dreadful is the check — intense the agony —
When the ear begins to hear, and the eye begins to see;
When the pulse begins to throb, the brain to think again;
The soul to feel the flesh, and the flesh to feel the chain.

Yet I would lose no sting, would wish no torture less;
The more that anguish racks, the earlier it will bless;
And robed in fires of hell, or bright with heavenly shine,
If it but herald death, the vision is divine!

EMILY JANE BRONTË
Poems (1846)

"The mystic attitude is not of calm control or angry revolt and self-assertion," D. S. MacColl (*Nineteenth Century Art,* 1902) remarks in what might be a gloss upon both Emily Brontë's poem and Rembrandt's painting. "It is a loss, a surrender of self in ecstatic contemplation, looking through the thing to something beyond it. Since things are signs of more than themselves to the mystic, he is often content with a symbol, the sign of a sign." Collections: Viscountess Hampder; J. A. Beaver, Lancashire; E. W. Parker, Skirwith Abbey, Cumberland; F. von Gans, Frankfort-on-Main. *Widener Collection,* 1942. Canvas. Height 56¼ in.; width 43¾ in. (1.43 x 1.11). Signed, and dated 165(1?).

JAN VERMEER · Dutch 1632-1675

The Girl with a Red Hat

But of Vermeer we know nothing save that he was a materialistic Dutchman who applied paint to canvas with a dexterity and charm that have never been equalled: in short, with perfection. His pictures tell us that he was not imaginative and not unhappy; they do not suggest any particular richness of personality: there is nothing in them or in his life to inspire a poet as Andrea and Lippo Lippi inspired Browning and as Romney inspired Tennyson. Vermeer was not like that.

But when it comes to perfection in the use of paint, when it comes to "The Perfect Painter" — why, here he is. His contemporary, Rembrandt of the Rhine (whose hand has been traced by the experts in nearly seven hundred paintings), is a giant beside him; but ruggedness was part of his strength. His contemporary, Franz Hals of Haarlem, could dip his brush in red and transform the pigment into pulsating blood with one flirt of his wrist; and yet think of his splendid carelessness elsewhere. His contemporary, Jan Steen of Leyden, had a way of kindling with a touch an eye so that it danced with vivacity and dances still, after all these years; but what a sloven he could be in his backgrounds! His contemporary, Peter de Hooch (to whom, as I have said, for two purblind centuries, Vermeer's pictures were chiefly attributed), could flood canvas with the light of the sun, but how weakly drawn are some of his figures! And so one might go on with the other great painters — the Italians and the Spanish and the English and the French, naming one after another, all with more to them as personalities than Vermeer, all doing more work, yet all, even Michelangelo and Leonardo, even Correggio, even Raphael, even Andrea, even Chardin (who was, so to speak, Vermeer's love-child), falling beneath him in the mere technical mastery of the brush and the palette — no one having with such accuracy and happiness adjusted the means to the desired end. Vermeer aimed low, but at his best he stands as near perfection as is possible.

E. V. Lucas
Vermeer of Delft (1922)

We know the present picture was purchased by Baron Atthalin in 1823 and remained in his family until recently. It may have been painted as a pendant to the Girl with a Flute. In both pictures the costume is fanciful. Therefore it is possible that this is the pair of pictures auctioned after Vermeer's death as heads in antique costume. If so, they must have parted company sometime after the sale, only to be reunited when Mr. Mellon gave one and Mr. Widener the other to the National Gallery of Art. Collections: Baron Atthalin and descendants. *Mellon Collection*, 1937. Wood. Height 9⅛ in.; width 7⅛ in. (0.232 x 0.181). Signed. Painted c. 1660.

AELBERT CUYP · Dutch 1620-1691

The Maas at Dordrecht

One of the first circumstances that struck me wherever I went was what you had prepared me for, the resemblance that every thing wore to the Dutch and Flemish pictures. On leaving Ostend, not only the people, the houses, and trees, but whole tracts of country, reminded one of the landscapes of Teniers; and, on getting further into the country, this was only relieved by the pictures of Rubens, Wouvermans, and some other masters, taking his place. I thought I could trace the particular districts in Holland where Ostade, Jan Stein, Cuyp, and Rembrandt had studied, and could fancy the very spot where pictures of other masters had been painted. Indeed, nothing seemed new to me in the whole country; for I had been familiar with it all upon canvas: and, what one could not help wondering at was, that these old masters should have been able to draw the materials of so beautiful a variety of art from so contracted and monotonous a country.

Sir David Wilkie
Letter to Sir George Beaumont (Dec. 12, 1816)

If I might point out to you another defect, very prevalent of late, in our pictures, and one of the same contracted character with those you so happily illustrate, it would be that of the *want of breadth,* and in others a perpetual division and subdivision of parts, to give what their perpetrators call space; add to this a constant disturbing and torturing of every thing, whether in light or in shadow, by a niggling touch, to produce fulness of subject. This is the very reverse of what we see in Cuyp or Wilson, and even, with all his high finishing, in Claude.

I have been warning our friend Collins against this, and was also urging young Landseer to beware of it; and in what I have been doing lately myself have been studying much from Rembrandt and from Cuyp, so as to acquire what the great masters succeeded so well in, namely, that power by which the chief objects, and even the minute finishing of parts, tell over every thing that is meant to be subordinate in their pictures. Sir Joshua had this remarkably, and could even make *the features of the face* tell over every thing, however strongly painted. I find that repose and breadth in the shadows and half-tints do a great deal towards it. Zoffany's figures derive great consequence from this; and I find that those who have studied light and shadow the most never appear to fail in it.

Sir David Wilkie
Letter to Sir George Beaumont (Feb. 14, 1823)

In the *Commemorative Catalogue of the Exhibition of Dutch Art, Burlington House,* 1929, it is suggested that "the event represented is probably Charles II in the Dordrecht roads, May 24th, 1660, during his journey from Breda . . . . to the Hague and thence to England." Collections: Alexis de la Hante; Sir Abraham Hume, and his descendants, until sold by Adelbert Wellington, 3rd Earl Brownlow, Ashridge Park, England. *Mellon Collection,* 1940. Canvas. Height 46¼ in.; width 67 in. (1.15 x 1.70). Signed. Painted c. 1660.

GERARD TER BORCH · DUTCH 1617-1681

The Suitor's Visit

I spent some time watching them, and soon saw the redshanks courting. It was one of the most entrancing of spectacles. Redshanks, cock as well as hen, are sober-coloured enough as you see their trim brown bodies slipping through the herbage. But during the courtship all is changed. The cock-bird advances towards the hen with his graceful pointed wings raised above his back, showing their pure-white under-surface. He lifts his scarlet legs alternately in a deliberate way — a sort of graceful goose-step — and utters all the while a clear far-carrying trill, full of wildness, charged with desire, piercing and exciting. Sometimes as he nears the hen he begins to fan his wings a little, just lifting himself off the ground, so that he is walking on air.

JULIAN HUXLEY
Bird-Watching and Bird Behaviour (1930)

Nearly all Ter Borch's pictures are interiors. He takes us into a Dutch room, where he shows only a bare wall, perhaps adorned with a map or interrupted by a fireplace. In the foreground. . . . are a carpet-covered table and one or two chairs. The figures, which are quiet and unemotional, are endowed with the same apparent plainness and simplicity. This extreme reserve, decidedly premeditated, is united with an unaffected grace and a certain grandeur, for which the choice garments and their fashionable styling are necessary conditions. It gives Ter Borch's pictures their air of distinction. Thanks to his unobtrusive, aristocratic manner and his cultured breeding the artist knows how to depict his countrymen in an aspect that none of his colleagues has shown us. He portrays them with a plausible cool dignity and elegance, but their society does not chill us; on the contrary, it arouses in us an intimate response, so that in this world of quiet and easy manners we feel at home. We are interested in what is going on and, with Goethe, are tempted to reconstruct the story.

WILHELM VON BODE
Die Meister der Holländischen und Vlämischen Malerschulen (1919)

Collections: Charles-Auguste-Louis-Joseph, Duc de Morny, Paris; Marqués de Salamanca, Madrid; Adolphe de Rothschild, Paris; Maurice de Rothschild, Paris. *Mellon Collection,* 1937. Canvas. Height 31½ in.; width 29⅝ in. (0.80 x 0.75). Painted 1660-70.

JACOB VAN RUISDAEL · Dutch 1628/29-1682

Forest Scene

Towards evening, Goethe invited me to take a drive. Our road lay over the hills through Upper Weimar, by which we had a view of the park towards the west. The trees were in blossom, the birches already in full leaf; and the meadows were one green carpet, over which the setting sun cast a glow. We sought out picturesque groups, and could not look enough. We remarked that trees full of white blossoms should not be painted, because they make no picture, just as birches with their foliage are unfit for the foreground of a picture, because the delicate leaf does not sufficiently balance the white trunk; there are no large masses for strong effects of light and shade. "Ruysdael," said Goethe, "never introduced the birch with its foliage into his foregrounds, but only birch trunks broken off, without any leaves. Such a trunk is perfectly suited to a foreground, as its bright form comes out with most powerful effect."

JOHANN PETER ECKERMANN
Gespräche mit Goethe (May 2, 1824)

As Babbitt (*Rousseau and Romanticism,* 1919) has pointed out, "Romanticism gave a great impulse to landscape painting" and the creed of the Romantic landscapist is expressed in Wordsworth's familiar lines:

> *One impulse from a vernal wood*
> *May teach you more of man,*
> *Of moral evil and of good,*
> *Than all the sages can.*

Images which would evoke these impulses "from a vernal wood" were established by the Dutch painters of the seventeenth century and became the basis of the landscape painting of the nineteenth century, as developed by Constable and Turner, by the Barbizon School, by the Impressionists and by many others. Collections: Sir Hugh Hume Campbell, London. *Widener Collection,* 1942. Canvas. Height 41½ in.; width 51½ in. (1.055 x 1.31). Painted c. 1660-65.

LOUIS LE NAIN · French c. 1593-1648

Landscape with Peasants

A painter of atmosphere, of light — in short, an impressionist — is he not an artist for whom the outside world counts more than his dreams, visualization more than conception? But Louis Le Nain is not an impressionist, because he has not taken *his* light and *his* air from without nor from the subject — he created them. Creation for him, as for the cubist, according to the aphorism of Georges Braque, is superior to vision. This landscape, as French as a landscape of Corot or of Cézanne, is so very French because of a spiritual quality shared by the figures, the expression, the entire work of art. The brightness does not come from the sun, but from within. It is, after all, only a reflection of a being who thinks, a category of understanding. Louis Le Nain did not pretend to paint the light of a moment, an hour, a season or a province, any more than Poussin and the classicists. Like them, he painted according to modes that correspond to certain classes of emotions and perceptions. Chardin, whose words should not be taken literally, said, "one makes use of color, one paints with feeling." It follows that while a Monet, for example, works unceasingly at pursuing the fugitive and changeable, Louis Le Nain, along with all those who are most deserving to be called French painters. . . . interprets the permanent aspect of beings and things in his own way. It is according to a disciplined method, a poetic and measured language — nature as he understands it, clarified, distilled.

"Nature is a dictionary," said Delacroix. Nature reviewed and corrected by Louis Le Nain is a world of stable forms, charged with a spiritual content that transcends the sometimes clumsy plot of the peasant anecdote. The central figures are silent; nevertheless, a majestic song arises from their gatherings.

Paul Fierens
Les Le Nain (1933)

The landscape by Louis Le Nain suggests the work of certain Neo-Romantics, especially Eugene Berman. The composition seems casual, almost fortuitous, compared with the highly intellectual and integrated designs of such classical artists as Nicolas Poussin (see page 112). Though Classicism dominated French taste in the seventeenth century, Louis Le Nain and his two brothers belonged to a school of naturalistic artists who imitated the Dutch genre style and were influenced by the work of Caravaggio. Thus they stand outside the main stream of the French painting of their time. Another version of this picture, with slight variations, is in the collection of the Duke of Westminster. Collections: Gainsborough (?), London; Dr. Dibdin; Joseph Neeld (?), London; Sir Audley Neeld, Chippenham, Wiltshire. *Samuel H. Kress Collection*, 1939. Canvas. Height 18⅜ in.; width 22½ in. (0.465 x 0.57). Painted c. 1640.

NICOLAS POUSSIN · French 1593/94-1665

The Baptism of Christ

The idea of beauty does not descend into matter unless this is prepared as carefully as possible. This preparation consists of three things: arrangement, measure, and aspect or form. Arrangement means the relative position of the parts; measure refers to their size; and form consists of lines and colors. Arrangement and relative position of the parts and making every limb of the body hold its natural place are not sufficient unless measure is added, which gives to each limb its correct size, proportionate to that of the whole body, and unless form joins in, so that the lines will be drawn with grace and with a harmonious juxtaposition of light and shadow.

From all the foregoing it can clearly be seen that beauty is altogether independent of the matter of the body, which never receives it unless it is predisposed with these incorporeal preparations. And here we may conclude that painting is nothing but an image of incorporeal things, despite the fact that it exhibits bodies, for it represents only the arrangements, proportions, and forms of things, and is more intent on the idea of beauty than on any other. Wherefore some have maintained that beauty alone is the mark and, as it were, the goal of all good painters, and that painting is the wooer of beauty and the queen of the arts.

NICOLAS POUSSIN
in G. P. Bellori, *Le Vite de' pittori, scultori et architetti moderni* (1672)

On the whole, Poussin followed the classical tradition, composing his paintings in planes parallel to the front of the picture, but he brought into equilibrium a more complicated arrangement of stresses and counter-stresses than Raphael, who was the source of his style. Poussin analyzed his designs by placing wax models on a miniature stage. This enabled him to render clearly the relationship between the volumes of separate figures. The Baptism is the last canvas executed in the series of The Seven Sacraments which the artist began about 1635 for Cassiano del Pozzo. Poussin's French patron Paul de Chantelou, after seeing the Baptism, ordered a duplication of the whole series, which was painted by Poussin, 1644-48, with much variation from the first series. This second series is now in the Bridgewater House Collection. On the authenticity of the above statements attributed to Poussin, see Anthony Blunt, *Journal of the Warburg Institute,* 1938. Collections: Cassiano del Pozzo, Rome; Marquis Bocca Paduli, Rome; Duke of Rutland, Belvoir Castle, Leicestershire (acquired 1786, along with the other paintings in the series, upon the advice of Sir Joshua Reynolds). *Samuel H. Kress Collection,* 1939. Canvas. Height 37⅝ in.; width 47⅝ in. (0.955 x 1.21). Painted 1641-42.

CLAUDE LORRAIN · French 1600-1682

The Herdsman

But when the west winds call and the exquisite warm season
Ushers them out, both sheep and goats, to glade and pasture,
At the first wink of the Morning Star let us wend away
To the frore fields, while the morning is young, the meadow pearly,
And dew so dear to cattle lies on the tender grass.
Then, when the fourth hour of the sun has created a thirst
And the plantations vibrate with the pizzicato of crickets,
I'll bring the flocks to water by wells and by deep ponds,
I'll bid them drink the water that runs in the troughs of ilex.
But now it's the noonday heat, make for a shady combe
Where some great ancient-hearted oak throws out its huge
Boughs, or the wood is black with
A wealth of holm-oak and broods in its own haunted shadow.
Then give them runnels of water again and let them browse
About sundown, when the cool star of evening assuages
The air, and moonlight falls now with dew to freshen the glades,
And the kingfisher's heard on the shore and the warbler in woody thickets.

VIRGIL
Georgics (29 B.C.)

West observed that Claude had so continued his lights that the eye always settled upon the distance & the Center of the picture,—as the eye naturally does in viewing the scenes of nature.—He remarked how carefully Claude had avoided sharp & decided forms in the distance, gradually *defining the* parts as He came nearer to the foreground.—He thinks Claude began his pictures by laying in simple gradations of flat colours from the Horizon to the top of the sky,—and from the Horizon to the foreground, witht. putting clouds into the sky or specific forms into the landscape till He had fully settled those gradations.—When He had satisfied himself in this respect, He painted in his forms, by that means securing a due gradation,—from the Horizontal line to the top of his Sky,— and from the Horizontal line to the foreground.—Smirke remarked how entirely all *positive* colour was avoided, even to the draperies of the figures.—Turner said He was both pleased & unhappy while He viewed it,—it seemed to be beyond the power of imitation.

JOSEPH FARINGTON
Diary (May 8, 1799)

For Latin text see page 183. Parallels between writers and painters are rarely as close as between Virgil and Claude. Landscape is imbued by Claude with all the tranquility and stillness of Virgil's summer day. Much of this painting's fascination for us depends on the sweep of space, the wash of air, the way the eye glides rapidly to distant mountains and headlands, effects that are caused by those subtle gradations of tone which West analyzes. Collections: Baron Gustave de Rothschild, Paris; Marquess of Cholmondeley, Houghton Hall, Norfolk, England. *Samuel H. Kress Collection*, 1939. Canvas. Height 47¾ in.; width 63⅛ in. (1.215 x 1.605). Painted probably 1655-60.

NICOLAS LANCRET · French 1690-1743

La Camargo Dancing

Death has just deprived us of two solitary virgins, of the royal Academy of Music, vulgarly called the Opera. They had long been dead to the stage, and their old age was honourably supported by the fruits of their youthful labours. The names of Camargo and Carton will be eternally celebrated in the commemorations of the Opera. Mademoiselle Camargo, sister to Cupis Violon, known by a thousand brilliant adventures behind the scenes, is immortalized at the theatre as the foundress of that stile of dancing with pirouettes, which has been brought in our days, to such perfection by Mademoiselle Allard. Camargo was the first woman who ventured to shorten her petticoats, so as to give amateurs an opportunity of passing their judgment upon the legs of the female dancers. Though this fashion has since been almost universally adopted, it occasioned, at the time, a very dangerous schism. The Jansenists, of the pit, cried out heresy and scandal, and would not suffer the shortened petticoats; but the Molinists, on the contrary, contended strenuously that this innovation carried us nearer to the primitive church, which was revolted at seeing pirouettes encumbered by the length of the petticoats. The Sorbonne of the Opera held a great many sittings before they could decide which of the contending parties adhered to the orthodox doctrine; but at length decided in favour of the short petticoat adherents, with a clause, however, that no female dancer should be permitted to come upon the stage without drawers. This decision has since become a fundamental article of discipline, by the general consent of all the ruling powers of the Opera.

I had the good fortune, upon my arrival in France, to find Camargo still upon the stage, though she was in the autumn of her career, indeed drawing towards the winter. She has lived since she quitted the theatre, in a peaceable and honourable retreat, surrounded by half a dozen dogs, and visited constantly by one friend whom she retained to the last from among her thousand and one lovers; her dogs are all bequeathed to him. He made a magnificent funeral for her, and every body admired the white ornaments, symbols of virginity, to which persons who have never been married, have a right at their interment. Since Camargo quitted the stage, the art of dancing, in all its branches, has made such a rapid progress, that her agility, which, at that time was thought so extraordinary, would now, by the side of Mademoiselle Allard and others, obtain only a moderate share of admiration. To have their names descend to posterity, it is necessary that a female dancer should have lived in the age of shortened petticoats.

FRIEDRICH MELCHIOR VON GRIMM
Correspondance littéraire (May, 1770)

Both poetry and painting record the success of La Camargo. With Mlle. Sallé she inspired Voltaire's enthusiastic eulogy that opens with the line: "Ah! Camargo, que vous êtes brillante!" Lancret painted her several times (Wallace Collection, Hermitage, Nantes) but only the present version shows her with her partner Laval. This is one of twenty-six pictures by Lancret remaining from the collection of Frederick the Great of Prussia. With many of the others it was in the palace at Potsdam until after the first World War. Collections: Prince de Carignan; Frederick the Great of Prussia; Wilhelm II of Germany. *Mellon Collection,* 1937. Canvas. Height 30 in.; width 42 in. (0.76 x 1.07). Painted c. 1730.

116

JEAN-MARC NATTIER · French 1685-1766

Madame de Caumartin as Hebe

In society one must give the appearance of living on ambrosia and of cherishing only noble thoughts. Care, need, passion are non-existent. All realism, being brutal, is suppressed. These goddesses are reputed to have descended from Olympus, and to be subject to none of the ills of this world. They no longer have any internal organs or any corpulence, they retain of the human body only what is necessary for grace and voluptuousness. In a word, the so-called *grand monde* is giving itself temporarily the flattering illusion of existing in an ethereal state, and of enjoying a mythological life. This is why any violence, any natural impulse, any true suffering, any heedless familiarity, any frank display of passion, shock and jar in this delicate *milieu*. Any coarseness immediately destroys the collective work, the cloud-palace, the wondrous architectural creation erected by common consent. It is like the shrill cockcrow that dissolves all enchantment and puts the fairies to flight. Select gatherings labor unaware to create a kind of concert for eye and ear, an improvised work of art. This instinctive collaboration possesses a real charm, for wit and taste hold court, and the actors are transported into the realm of imagination. It is a form of poetry, and it is thus that cultivated society deliberately resurrects a vanished idyll and the engulfed world of Astraea. Paradox or no, I believe that these fleeting attempts to reconstruct a dream dedicated only to beauty represent confused remembrances of a golden age which haunt the human heart, or rather aspirations toward a harmonious existence denied us in daily life, and of which art alone gives us a glimpse.

Henri Frédéric Amiel
Journal intime (Feb. 22, 1871)

Madame de Caumartin was the wife of an official who served as Prévôt des Marchands in Paris. The Hebe motif, suggesting eternal youth, was made popular by Nattier in 1745 with his portraits of the future Duchess of Orleans and others of rank. "One might well think," writes Cochin, a contemporary critic, concerning the ladies of his day, "that one of their principal pastimes was raising birds, even the most difficult to tame, such as eagles, to which they gave white wine in golden cups." In the portrait of the Duchess of Orleans, now in the Stockholm Museum, the composition, costume and accessories are, in spite of having been painted eight years earlier, almost the same as in the present painting. Collections: Comtesse de Gramont d'Aster; Comtesse Louis de Montesquiou; Comtesse Fleury. *Samuel H. Kress Collection*, 1939. Canvas. Height 40⅜ in.; width 32 in. (1.025 x 0.815). Signed, and dated 1753.

JEAN-BAPTISTE PATER · French 1695-1736

Fête Champêtre

By *fête galante* is not necessarily meant a licentious or erotic scene, . . . but something similar to a profane *santa conversazione*: a gathering of elegant cavaliers and their lovely companions who chat or enjoy music in the park. This genre is an exquisite flower of a refined and leisurely era when seemingly life's goal was to flirt and to listen to the rustling of leaves and the dulcet harmonies of flutes and viols, while stretched out carelessly on the grass.

Louis Réau
Histoire de la peinture française au XVIIIᵉ siècle (1925)

Pour faire au Cours des conquêtes nouvelles
            L'Amour attire tout Paris;
            Au clair de la Lune les Belles
            Changent souvent de Favoris,
            Et ne sont gueres plus fidelles
            A leurs Amans qu'à leurs Maris.

Jeunes Fillettes
            Dissimulez
Les ardeurs secrettes
            Dont vous brûlez;
Quand sous son Empire
Le Dieu des amours
A sçû vous réduire,
Cachez bien toûjours
Ce qu'il vous inspire,
Ou si son martire
Vous force à le dire,
Laissez-vous conduire
Aux Fêtes du Cours.

Beautez qui voulez qu'on vous aime,
            Pourquoi vous défendre d'aimer?
            Il est mal aisé d'allumer
Les feux d'amour sans en brûler soi-même.

Florent Carton Dancourt
Les Festes nocturnes du cours (1714)

For translation see page 183. French painting in the eighteenth century gained the hegemony that it has held ever since in European art. Rubens had supplanted Raphael as the model to emulate; and the resulting change in design can be understood by contrasting Poussin's Baptism (page 113) with Pater's Fête Champêtre. Poussin's construction is that of an engineer who balances thrust against thrust to establish an equilibrium; Pater's is that of a musician who takes a theme, in this case the curve of the volute on the left, and repeats it with variations through the whole composition. Thus the groups of figures and the masses of foliage in the Fête Champêtre all lean and sway to the same dominant rhythm. The composition of this picture is closely paralleled in a painting by Pater in the Wallace Collection, London, where the group of two children with a dog is almost exactly repeated. Collections: Baroness Wilhelm von Rothschild. *Samuel H. Kress Collection*, 1939. Canvas. Height 29⅜ in.; width 36½ in. (0.745 x 0.925). Painted c. 1730.

JEAN-BAPTISTE-SIMEON CHARDIN · French 1699-1779

The House of Cards

All art exhibits connection, a bringing together. In visual art alone, and then solely in visual art deeply founded upon this colour-cum-architectural sense of form, an aesthetic communication may be explicit and immediate to the point of rebutting after-thought. It is the *réaliser* of Cézanne. Such demonstration of intellect and feeling was the crown of the *Quattro Cento* compulsion to make manifest. Thereafter the same chromatic sense of form to some degree persisted in post-Renaissance art refurbished, if we consider painting only, by Vermeer, for instance, by Chardin, re-enacted by Cézanne. Yet there has not been, and still there is lacking, a generalized apprehension of this side of visual art, eminent not only in painting but also in drawing, in sculpture and more particularly, in architecture whose steadfast forms and textures (not colours) have so often endowed that sensibility with archetypes. . . .

There can be no art without something, however minute, of this quality; because Art, mirror of each aim, conspires to win for expression the finality of death.

ADRIAN STOKES
Art and Science (1949)

This painting is considered to be the earliest of Chardin's several versions of the theme, the most important of which are in the following collections: Viscount Harcourt, Nuneham Park, England; Oskar Reinhardt, Winterthur, Switzerland; Louvre, Paris; Henri de Rothschild, Paris; National Gallery, London. Engraved in reverse in the eighteenth century by P. A. Aveline. Collections: Hermitage Gallery, Leningrad. *Mellon Collection,* 1937. Canvas. Height 32⅜ in.; width 26 in. (0.822 x 0.66). Painted probably 1735.

JEAN-HONORE FRAGONARD · FRENCH 1732-1806

A Game of Horse and Rider

Here, rather than in any bacchanal or ostentation of nudes, the fastidious voluptuary may find the life of which he dreams and of which he must always be frustrated. Nymphs as witty as they are seductive and kind; youthful gallants to whom these with a wise intuition prefer him; actors and singers to fan or to renew his flame; marionettes to reassure him that life is but a comedy, in case some grave reflection break in for a moment upon his errands. The painter has devised a Nature in gauze and feathers, a millinery of trees, under which to be private, and yet so little removed that the music will drift through the shadows to attend the grateful libation. Nor need one be at the bother of kissing. On these ample lawns those who prefer can indulgently elude the Paphian crew, and abandon themselves to the lazier cult of pretty memories.

Without the melancholy of Watteau, Fragonard yet knows that a touch of sentiment is becoming to the lightest loves; without Boucher's cynicism, Fragonard is just for this reason more masterly in provocation. "Oh, to have lived when frivolity could be thus poetical," sighs the modern rake—but it never was. A junketing at Saint-Cloud, which no doubt could be charming enough, has been turned to a vision of Armida's Garden.

RAYMOND MORTIMER
The Desirable Life
The Arts (1946)

In the eighteenth century, though the monarchy remained a source of patronage of art, it was only one of many. Commissions came very largely from wealthy Parisian amateurs, like the Baron de Saint-Julien, who commissioned this picture as well as its pendant, A Game of Hot Cockles, also in the National Gallery of Art, and The Swing, in the Wallace Collection, London. With such collectors a new genre, the *fête galante,* invented by Watteau, was popular; and as the century progressed, under the leadership of Fragonard, the emphasis in such pictures shifted from aristocratic to pastoral charm. Scenes of country junketing, so similar to Marie-Antoinette's bucolic episode at the Petit Trianon, appealed to a society enamoured of Rousseau and eager to return to nature and a rustic life. Collections: Baron de Saint-Julien; William Hope; Jenny Colon; E. Péreire; Comte Pillet-Will, Paris. *Samuel H. Kress Collection,* 1939. Canvas. Height 45⅜ in.; width 34½ in. (1.15 x 0.875). Painted between 1767 and 1773.

FRANÇOIS BOUCHER · FRENCH 1703-1770

Allegory of Music

Three types of men have made all beautiful things. Aristocracies have made beautiful manners, because their place in the world puts them above the fear of life, and the countrymen have made beautiful stories and beliefs, because they have nothing to lose and so do not fear, and the artists have made all the rest, because Providence has filled them with recklessness. All these look backward to a long tradition, for, being without fear, they have held to whatever pleased them. The others being always anxious have come to possess little that is good in itself, and are always changing from thing to thing, for whatever they do or have must be a means to something else, and they have so little belief that anything can be an end in itself, that they cannot understand you if you say, 'All the most valuable things are useless.' They prefer the stalk to the flower, and believe that painting and poetry exist that there may be instruction, and love that there may be children, and theatres that busy men may rest, and holidays that busy men may go on being busy. At all times they fear and even hate the things that have worth in themselves, for that worth may suddenly, as it were a fire, consume their book of Life, where the world is represented by cyphers and symbols; and before all else, they fear irreverent joy and unserviceable sorrow. It seems to them, that those who have been freed by position, by poverty, or by the traditions of Art, have something terrible about them, a light that is unendurable to eyesight. They complain much of that commandment that we can do almost what we will, if we do it gaily, and think that freedom is but a trifling with the world.

WILLIAM BUTLER YEATS
Poetry and Tradition (1907)

There are three things I have always loved and never understood — painting, music and women.

Attributed to BERNARD DE FONTENELLE

This canvas, together with its companion piece, Allegory of Painting, also in the National Gallery of Art, Samuel H. Kress Collection, is traditionally believed to have been painted for Maximilian-Joseph, the Elector of Bavaria who distinguished himself by his patronage of the sciences, letters and arts. There are similar compositions of an earlier date, the Muse of Poetry and the Muse of History, both in the Wallace Collection, London. Collections: Elector of Bavaria; General of Saint-Maurice; Maillet du Boulet; Rothan; Mme. Livingston-Sampson, Duchess of Dino; Count Orlowski. *Samuel H. Kress Collection,* 1939. Canvas. Height 40¾ in.; width 51⅛ in. (1.035 x 1.30). Signed, and dated 1764.

ELISABETH VIGEE-LEBRUN · French 1755-1842

Portrait of a Lady

In so far as the intellectual climates of different epochs can be contrasted, the eighteenth century in Europe was the complete antithesis to the Middle Ages. The contrast is symbolised by the difference between the cathedral of Chartres and the Parisian salons, where D'Alembert conversed with Voltaire. The Middle Ages were haunted with the desire to rationalise the infinite: the men of the eighteenth century rationalised the social life of modern communities, and based their sociological theories on an appeal to the facts of nature. The earlier period was the age of faith, based upon reason. In the later period, they let sleeping dogs lie: it was the age of reason, based upon faith. To illustrate my meaning: — St. Anselm would have been distressed if he had failed to find a convincing argument for the existence of God, and on this argument he based his edifice of faith, whereas Hume based his *Dissertation on the Natural History of Religion* upon his faith in the order of nature. In comparing these epochs it is well to remember that reason can err, and that faith may be misplaced.

ALFRED NORTH WHITEHEAD
Science and the Modern World (1925)

To compare Vigée-Lebrun's portrait with Chartres Cathedral is to put the former at an evident disadvantage. Nevertheless the painting exhibits as directly as may be the characteristic romanticism of the eighteenth century which Whitehead describes. At the same time, although the portrait comes at the end of the century, it stands for a romanticism that has not yet degenerated into the dreadful colloquialism of some of Wordsworth's poetry and the paintings that tended to fill the Salons of the next century. Collections: Mrs. Lyne Stephens (née Duvernay), London; John Pierpont Morgan, New York. *Samuel H. Kress Collection,* 1939. Wood. Height 42⅛ in.; width 32¾ in. (1.07 x 0.83). Inscribed with the artist's name, and dated 1789.

GOYA · Spanish 1746-1828

Señora Sabasa Garcia

Many of his portraits he painted in a single day, a sitting not of a few hours merely, but one that lasted the whole of the day, during which time Goya, inexorable towards his model, worked in absolute silence with extraordinary concentration and vigour.

His palette was of the simplest, and he was in the habit of painting at some distance from his sitter, attacking the masses broadly in monochrome, and once his planes and proportions were thoroughly well established, he worked in colour where it was needed. It must not, however, be imagined that all his portraits were attacked in a breathless manner. . . .

But the restlessness of his temperament made him inclined to seize on a characteristic rendering of pose and feature. A Miss Linley Goya could not give us, but something very like the delicate wantonness of a Perdita we may discover in more than one of his canvasses. He delighted in the very particular beauty of Spanish women; in their proud manner of walking, of wearing a mantilla, a flower; in their elaborate fashion of dressing the hair. He never tired of painting the high-heeled Moorish-pointed shoes in vogue in his day among Spanish ladies. A favourite method was to paint them seated, holding themselves very erect from the hips, almost *cambré*. . . .

"A picture, the effect of which is true, is finished," was a favourite dictum of his which has been applied since in a sense different, perhaps, to his meaning. For by this he meant not only truth of line, tone, or colour, but also truth of movement and emotion, of observation, in fact. As with Daumier and Millet, his sense of form was creative, as well as imitative, and like these he was able to produce an absolutely convincing effect, through his knowledge and intuition, where a more careful and conscientious artist would fail; and it is this imagination for reality, this power to render nature dramatically and impressively, that makes of him one of the most significant artists of the last two hundred years. The humanity grafted on to the tree of beauty by the gentle Rembrandt, was cultivated by Goya in a more critical and aggressive spirit; for he was not only the greatest painter of his age in Spain, but also the most fearless and advanced thinker.

William Rothenstein
Goya (1901)

According to a family tradition, Goya first saw the sitter, who was then eighteen, when he was painting her uncle, Don Evaristo Pérez de Castro, later Prime Minister of Spain. Attracted by her charm, he asked to paint her portrait. He executed the painting apparently with great rapidity and without changing a brush stroke, and presented it to her. In deftness of touch and brilliance of technique it anticipates Goya's later style. Collections: James Simon, Berlin. *Mellon Collection*, 1937. Canvas. Height 28 in.; width 23 in. (0.71 x 0.58). Probably painted shortly before 1808.

THOMAS GAINSBOROUGH · BRITISH 1727-1788

Landscape with a Bridge

Gainsborough . . . . gave up direct painting, and evolved the melodious style of picture making by which he is best known. His recent biographers have thought that the business of portrait painting left him no time to make studies from nature, and they have quoted his famous letter about being 'sick of portraits and wishing to take his Viol de Gamba and walk off to some sweet village where he can paint landskips' to support the view that he would have been a naturalistic landscape painter if he had had the opportunity. But the Viol de Gamba letter is only a part of Gainsborough's Rousseauism. His real opinions on the subject are contained in a letter to a patron who had been so simple as to ask him for a painting of his park: 'Mr. Gainsborough presents his humble respects to Lord Hardwicke, and shall always think it an honor to be employ'd in anything for His Lordship; but with regard to *real views* from Nature in this country, he has never seen any place that affords a subject equal to the poorest imitations of Gasper or Claude. Paul San[d]by is the only Man of Genius, he believes, who has employ'd his pencil that way. Mr. G. hopes Lord Hardwicke will not mistake his meaning, but if His Lordship wishes to have anything tollerable of the name of G., the subject altogether, as well as figures, etc., must be of his own Brain; otherwise Lord Hardwicke will only pay for encouraging a man out of his way, and had much better buy a picture of some of the good Old Masters.'

KENNETH CLARK
Landscape into Art (1949)

Why does a virtuous man take delight in landscapes? It is for these reasons: that in a rustic retreat he may nourish his nature; that amid the carefree play of streams and rocks, he may take delight; that he may constantly meet in the country fishermen, woodcutters, and hermits, and see the soaring of the cranes, and hear the crying of the monkeys. The din of the dusty world and the locked-in-ness of human habitations are what human nature habitually abhors; while, on the contrary, haze, mist, and the haunting spirits of the mountains are what human nature seeks, and yet can rarely find. When, however, in the heyday of great peace and prosperity, the minds, both of a man's sovereign and of his parents, are full of high expectations of his services, should he still stand aloof, neglecting the responsibilities of honour and righteousness? In the face of such duties the benevolent man cannot seclude himself and shun the world. . . .

Having no access to the landscapes, the lover of forest and stream, the friend of mist and haze, enjoys them only in his dreams. How delightful then to have a landscape painted by a skilled hand! Without leaving the room, at once, he finds himself among the streams and ravines.

KUO HSI
Lin Ch'üan Kao Chih (11th Century)

The rapid and sketchy execution of the picture is characteristic of the landscape work done by Gainsborough during the last years of his life. Such scenes are purely imaginative, and it is said that Gainsborough conceived them sitting at a table covered with lumps of coal and bits of moss, which he observed under different illuminations. The originality of his interpretation of nature had little appeal for collectors, and at Gainsborough's death his house was filled with unsold landscapes. Collections: Viscount d'Abernon, Esher (near London). *Mellon Collection*, 1937. Canvas. Height 44½ in.; width 52½ in. (1.13 x 1.33). Painted 1780-88.

SIR JOSHUA REYNOLDS · British 1723-1792

Lady Elizabeth Delmé and Her Children

Though Sir Joshua borrowed a great deal, he drew largely from himself: or rather, it was a strong and peculiar feeling of nature working in him and forcing its way out in spite of all impediments, and that made whatever he touched his own. In spite of his deficiency in drawing, and his want of academic rules and a proper education, you see this breaking out like a devil in all his works. It is this that has stamped him. There is a charm in his portraits, a mingled softness and force, a grasping at the end with nothing harsh or unpleasant in the means, that you will find nowhere else. He may go out of fashion for a time: but you must come back to him again, while a thousand imitators and academic triflers are forgotten. This proves him to have been a real genius. The same thing, however, made him a very bad master. He knew nothing of rules which are alone to be taught; and he could not communicate his instinctive feeling of beauty or character to others. I learnt nothing from him while I was with him: and none of his scholars (if I may except myself) ever made any figure at all. He only gave us his pictures to copy. Sir Joshua undoubtedly got his first ideas of the art from Gandy, though he lost them under Hudson; but he easily recovered them afterwards. That is a picture of Gandy's there (pointing to a portrait of a little girl). If you look into it, you will find the same broken surface and varying outline, that was so marked a characteristic of Sir Joshua. There was nothing he hated so much as a distinct outline, as you see it in Mengs and the French school. Indeed, he ran into the opposite extreme; but it is one of the great beauties of art to show it waving and retiring, now losing and then recovering itself again, as it always does in nature. without any of that stiff, edgy appearance, which only pedants affect or admire.

JAMES NORTHCOTE
In conversation

In nature color exists no more than line; there is only light and shade. Give me a piece of charcoal and I will make you a picture.

GOYA
In conversation

It is a paradox of the history of painting that though Reynolds was, as Northcote says, a very bad teacher, his *Discourses* remain the masterpiece of English art criticism. For he had a mind disciplined by his friendship with Doctor Johnson and a knowledge of the schools of painting gained by his indefatigable sightseeing. Cunningham (*Lives of the Most Eminent British Painters, Sculptors, and Architects,* 1829) points out that Reynolds' greatest contribution was his effect "on the taste and elegance of the Island." In England "the rich and the well-descended were pleased to be painted by a gentleman as well as a genius." Reynolds' portraits have increased in fashion till quite recently. Though in his lifetime he received only some £150 for a full-length portrait, even a contemporary mezzotint of Lady Elizabeth Delmé sold as high as £1,000 in the early part of this century. Today Reynolds' mezzotints and paintings alike have declined to a fraction of their value of a generation ago, for elegance has lost its popularity. Collections: the family of the sitter; Charles John Wertheimer, London; John Pierpont Morgan, New York. *Mellon Collection,* 1937. Canvas. Height 94 in.; width 58⅛ in. (2.49 x 1.475). Painted 1777-80.

GEORGE ROMNEY · British 1734-1802

Miss Willoughby

What is it, then, that gives Romney his hold upon this generation, and will continue to give him a hold so long as a love of art endures among us? In part, of course, it is because he shares with Reynolds and Gainsborough the good fortune of having kept alive for us a society of which the fascination is enduring—that limited and privileged society of the eighteenth century, which had realised such a perfect art of living, and with which we can clasp hands across the gulf, as we cannot with the men and women of Charles the Second's time, or even of Queen Anne's. Much more is it because, by temperament and training, Romney was an artist in love with loveliness; because he found it in the women and children of his time, and stamped it on countless canvases. To our problem-haunted painters of to-day, it may seem that his sense of form, as [D. S. MacColl] has said, was "generic and superficial"; they may condemn him because he did not try to penetrate deep into character, and because he simplified too much, like the Greek sculptors. The lover of mere human beauty will care little for such objections.... Again, our lover of beauty finds his satisfaction—and here the most exacting painter-critic will be at one with him—in the "large and unfrittered design" which is the mark of almost every mature Romney without exception. Of all his natural gifts this was the greatest; it was because he was a born designer that he found such pleasure and stimulus in the Stanze of the Vatican; that he surrounded himself with fine casts from the antique, and "would sit and consider these in profound silence by the hour."

HUMPHRY WARD AND WILLIAM ROBERTS
Romney (1904)

Whether owing to some unconjectured and innate vanity in the English character, or merely to a puritan distrust of art except in its more concrete expressions, portraiture had ever, historically, been the manifestation of it which, since the Reformation, the English patron had favoured. To saints, angels, and martyrs, pagan deities and mythological heroes, he paid but little attention: his own face, and those of his numerous progeny, were all that he considered necessary, in the way of beauty, to perpetuate for the applause of an astonished posterity. This tendency had been further encouraged by the generous patronage accorded to Vandyke by Charles I. Thus portraiture had become established as the one English manifestation of pictorial art and long remained its chief duty and only remunerative branch. Indeed from the day of Vandyke onward, money, much money, and not a little fame, could be earned by the painter who adopted it as his whole profession.

OSBERT SITWELL AND MARGARET BARTON
in *Johnson's England* (1933)

Whether or not one agrees with Sitwell and Barton in considering portraiture "the one English manifestation of pictorial art," it should be added that the English School made of portrait painting an art of decoration. Often weak in likeness and characterization, English portraits are almost always beautifully designed to harmonize with the graceful lines of Georgian architecture. They appear at their best, therefore, in eighteenth-century rooms, where their compositions echo and reinforce the subtle, elusive rhythms of Chippendale and Hepplewhite interiors. Collections: Major Sir John Christopher Willoughby, Fulmer Hall, Slough, Buckinghamshire. *Mellon Collection*, 1937. Canvas. Height 36⅛ in.; width 28 in. (0.918 x 0.71). Painted 1781-83, when the sittings were recorded in the artist's diaries.

GILBERT STUART · American 1755-1828

The Skater

We now come to No. 190, *Portrait of a Gentleman Skating,* the exhibition of which was the real beginning of Stuart's success in London, when, as he told Josiah Quincy many years afterwards, he was "suddenly lifted into fame by a single picture." The success of this portrait (of Mr. Grant of Congalton) was, however, hardly so great as Stuart implies. Nor is there, I think, any foundation for the story the artist Fraser told Dunlap, that so much attention was attracted to it at the Academy that when Mr. Grant went there and was recognized as the original of the portrait he was so mobbed by the crowd that he was compelled to leave the gallery. . . .

Recalling in 1795 his achievement of 1782, [a London critic] remarks:

> It is now some years since Stuart the portrait painter, who is now in New York, painted the portrait of a Mr. Grant in the action of skating; this portrait was given in so spirited an attitude and with so appropriate a character that when exhibited, it established the fame of the artist, of whom his brethren had before that time said he made a tolerable likeness of a face but as to the figure he could not get below the fifth button.

Little did Stuart dream in 1782 that his skating portrait would be shown again at the Royal Academy nearly a century later, to be an object of general admiration and the theme of discussions and disputes as to its authorship by the connoisseurs and critics of that day.

WILLIAM T. WHITLEY
Gilbert Stuart (1932)

English nineteenth-century art critics forgot the existence of Stuart and attributed this painting to Gainsborough. Other paintings by Stuart were attributed to Raeburn and Romney. The subject of the portrait is William Grant of Congalton, East Lothian, Scotland. According to Lawrence Park (*Gilbert Stuart*, 1926) the day appointed for the first sitting was very cold, and Mr. Grant remarked that the weather seemed more suitable for skating than for painting portraits. Portraitist and sitter thereupon went off to the frozen Serpentine, and this gave Stuart the idea of painting Mr. Grant in the act of skating. Collections: Inherited by William Grant's daughter, through whose marriage it came into the Pelham-Clinton family, Moor Park, Stroud, Gloucestershire, and London, in whose possession it remained until 1950. *Mellon Collection*, 1950. Canvas. Height 96⅝ in.; width 58⅛ in. (2.453 x 1.476). Painted 1782.

THOMAS SULLY · AMERICAN 1783-1872

Lady with a Harp: Eliza Ridgely

There is a species of female beauty almost peculiar to this country. Perhaps it is best described as the very opposite of robust. Indeed, it is winsome partly from the sense of fragility it conveys. Lightness of figure, delicacy of feature, and a transparent complexion are its essentials. It is suggestive at once of that quality which the French call *spirituelle;* and we can readily account for the partiality it excites in foreigners, from their having been accustomed to the hearty attractions of the Anglo-Saxons, or the noble outline and impassioned expression of the southern Europeans. It is an acknowledged fact, that the physical development of American women is precocious, and the decay of their charms premature. The variability of our climate, the want of regular exercise in the open air, and the harassing responsibilities they so early assume, too often unrelieved by wholesome pastime, are some of the reasons assigned for this state of things; explained as it may be, however, these characteristics of American beauty are visible all around us; and to arrest graces so ethereal, and truly embody them, requires somewhat of poetry as well as skill in an artist. If ever there was a man specially endowed to delineate our countrywomen, particularly those of the northern and middle States — where the peculiarities we have noticed are chiefly observable, it is Thomas Sully. His organization fits him to sympathize with the fair and lovely, rather than the grand and comic. He is keenly alive to the more refined phases of life and nature. His pencil follows with instinctive truth, the principles of genuine taste. He always seizes upon the redeeming element, and avails himself of the most felicitous combinations. Sully's forte is the graceful. Whatever faults the critics may detect in his works, they are never those of awkwardness or constraint. He exhibits the freedom of touch and the airiness of outline which belong to spontaneous emanations. Indeed, his defect, comparatively speaking, lies in this fairy-like, unsubstantial manner. Many of his female portraits strike us as "too wise and good," too like "creatures of the element," to be loved or blamed. Some of them float before the gaze like spirits of the air, or peer from a shadowy canvas like enchanted ladies. They are half-celestial, and we tremble, lest they should disappear as we gaze.

HENRY T. TUCKERMAN
Artist-Life (1847)

Judging by the payment recorded by Sully in his account book, this portrait was one of the most important commissions he received. The sitter was Mrs. John Ridgely, née Elizabeth Eichelberger Ridgely, who married a distant cousin, John Ridgely, in 1828. He was a son of Governor Charles Ridgely, of Hampton, Maryland, where the painting remained until acquired for the National Gallery of Art. Contrast the ideal of feminine beauty described by Tuckerman with the painting of Madame Moitessier (see page 147). *Gift of Mrs. Maude Monell Vetlesen*, 1945. Canvas. Height 84⅜ in.; width 56⅛ in. (2.145 x 1.425). Painted 1848.

140

JOHN CONSTABLE · British 1776-1837

A View of Salisbury Cathedral

The process of artistic creation would be better described as a process of discovery and disentanglement. To use the metaphor which one is by now so familiar with—the stream of the inner life, and the definite crystallised shapes on the surface—the big artist, the creative artist, the innovator, leaves the level where things are crystallised out into these definite shapes, and, diving down into the inner flux, comes back with a new shape which he endeavours to fix. He cannot be said to have created it, but to have discovered it, because when he has definitely expressed it we recognise it as true. Great painters are men in whom has originated a certain vision of things which has become or will become the vision of everybody. Once the painter has seen it, it becomes easy for all of us to see it. A mould has been made. But the creative activity came in the effort which was necessary to disentangle this particular type of vision from the general haze—the effort, that is, which is necessary to break moulds and to make new ones.

For instance, the effect produced by Constable on the English and French Schools of landscape painting. Nobody before Constable saw things, or at any rate painted them, in that particular way. This makes it easier to see clearly what one means by an individual way of looking at things. It does not mean something which is peculiar to an individual, for in that case it would be quite valueless. It means that a certain individual artist was able to break through the conventional ways of looking at things which veil reality from us at a certain point, was able to pick out one element which is really in all of us, but which before he had disentangled it, we were unable to perceive. It is as if the surface of our mind was a sea in a continual state of motion, that there were so many waves on it, their existence was so transient, and they interfered so much with each other, that one was unable to perceive them.

The artist by making a fixed model of one of these transient waves enables you to isolate it out and to perceive it in yourself. In that sense art merely reveals, it never creates.

T. E. HULME
Speculations (1924)

Constable's problem, almost never completely solved, was to convey to his finished pictures the emotion aroused by his first impression of a scene. Certain studies, painted in the process of arriving at the final exhibition pictures, hold a delicate balance between the spontaneity of the first idea and the too precise definition of the final version. The picture reproduced is one of many paintings of a motif that inspired some of Constable's most popular canvases. It is carried to a point, one feels, beyond which deterioration would commence. Collections: Sir John William Kelk, Wiltshire. *Mellon Collection*, 1937. Canvas. Height 28¾ in.; width 36 in. (0.73 x 0.91). Painted 1820-30.

J. M. W. TURNER · British 1775-1851

The Junction of the Thames and the Medway

Here was lately a cross-grained miser, odd and ugly, resembling in countenance the portrait of Punch with the laugh left out; rich by his own industry; sulking in a lonely house; who never gave a dinner to any man and disdained all courtesies: yet as true a worshipper of beauty in form and color as ever existed, and profusely pouring over the cold mind of his countrymen creations of grace and truth, removing the reproach of sterility from English art, catching from their savage climate every fine hint, and importing into their galleries every tint and trait of sunnier cities and skies; making an era in painting; and when he saw that the splendor of one of his pictures in the Exhibition dimmed his rival's that hung next it, secretly took a brush and blackened his own.

RALPH WALDO EMERSON
English Traits (1883)

Turner pierced through the bewildering accidents of growth down to character, to a system of curve or cleavage. . . .

To conquer the anatomy and architecture of clouds as well as of stationary rock and tree was a feat wonderful enough, but to surprise an intricate rhythm in the welter of waves, to wreathe a sculpture out of the waste wrath and torment of the sea, was his supreme triumph. The leap from the Dutch machine-made waves to these whelming and majestic living forms seems measurable by a difference in kind rather than degree of faculty; and features of translucency, pitch of lighting, foam-lace, elaborated by later painters, are minor curiosities compared with the coiling of Turner's wave.

With a tradition thus enriched and extended, Turner from 1800 to 1820 is again and again one of the most perfect of painters. . . . In this period he paints mountain and sea as Rembrandt painted humanity, with the same sculpturesque solidity of anatomy firmly grasped, the same wary, infinitely flexible hand for form, so that the eye is surprised and satisfied by every touch, the same rich, beautiful pastes of paint, fluid or 'short' as the texture of things demands, the same infinity in simplicity, so that one can watch the elusive pattern in the coiling of his waves close like a tune and yet escape and continue like moving nature, even as one can watch for a morning the growing of a feature out of a face in Rembrandt's portraits. As Rembrandt the face of a man, so Turner paints the side of a ship or of a hill with an aspect of drama, of long-suffering, of much living under the visit, the welling out, the majestic benediction of light.

D. S. MacColl
Nineteenth Century Art (1902)

There is a small version of this composition in the Ashmolean Museum, Oxford, and a pen-and-ink sketch in Turner's "Hesperides" sketchbook. Collections: John Newington Hughes, Winchester; Joseph Gillott, Birmingham; Richard Hemming, London. *Widener Collection*, 1942. Canvas. Height 42¾ in.; width 56 in. (1.085 x 1.42). Painted c. 1805-08.

JEAN-AUGUSTE-DOMINIQUE INGRES · French 1780-1867

Madame Moitessier

This confounded Realism made an immediate appeal to my painter's vanity, and, scoffing at all traditions, cried loudly with the confidence of ignorance, "Long live Nature!" *Nature,* my dear friend, is a watchword that has caused me much sorrow. Where could one have found an apostle readier to accept this convenient doctrine, this sedative for all misgivings? What! The painter had only to open his eyes and paint whatever was in front of him, beautiful Nature and all that goes with it! It was as easy as that! Very well, the world would see! And it saw *The Piano, The White Girl, The Thames,* seascapes . . . . canvases, in short, turned out by a rascal puffed up by the vanity of having the chance to exhibit to his fellow painters his magnificent gifts, talents which would have needed only a rigorous training to have made their possessor a master, at this very moment, and not a misguided tyro. Ah, my friend, our small band has indeed been a vicious society! Oh, that I had been a pupil of Ingres! I do not say that out of enthusiasm for his pictures. I have only a moderate liking for them. I find that several of his canvases, which we have looked at together, are of a very uncertain style, not at all Greek as people wish to call it, but very imperfectly French. I feel that we must go far beyond this, that there are far more beautiful things to be done. But — let me repeat — how I wish I had been his pupil! What a master he would have been! How salutary would have been his guidance!

JAMES A. McNEILL WHISTLER
Letter to Henri Fantin-Latour (1867)

It was once confessed to me, by a painter, that no professor of his art ever loved another.

SAMUEL JOHNSON
The Rambler (Oct. 27, 1750)

Ideals in feminine beauty change almost as rapidly as fashions in dress. Ingres reintroduced the canon of the sixteenth century, the requisites of which are described by the Swiss critic Wölfflin as a firm chin and full cheeks, a low forehead, eyebrows forming a straight line, a classic nose, and, above all, a mature, fully developed woman. Madame Moitessier fits this description admirably. She was a beauty Raphael or any painter of the High Renaissance would have admired (see page 64). With the revival of classicism in the nineteenth century regular and somewhat heavy features had again become fashionable, and Madame Moitessier was considered by Gautier and others as one of the most beautiful women of her generation. For a different ideal which, according to Tuckerman, was favored by American taste, see page 140, in connection with Eliza Ridgely's portrait, which was painted only three years before Madame Moitessier's was completed. Collections: Comtesse de Flavigny; Vicomtesse de Bondy; Comte Olivier de Bondy, Château de la Barre (Indre). *Samuel H. Kress Collection,* 1939. Canvas. Height 58¼ in.; width 40 in. (1.48 x 1.015). Painted 1851.

EUGENE DELACROIX · French 1798-1863

Columbus and His Son at La Rábida

What an adoration I have for painting! The mere memory of certain pictures, even when I don't see them, goes through me with a feeling which stirs my whole being like all those rare and interesting memories that one finds at long intervals in one's life, and especially in the very early years of it. . . .

The impressions produced by the arts on sensitive organisms are a curious mystery: confused impressions, if one tries to describe them, clear-cut and full of strength if one feels them again, and if only through memory! I strongly believe that we always mix in something of ourselves with feelings which seem to come from the objects that strike us. It is probable that the only reason why these works please me so much is that they respond to feelings which are my own; and since they give me the same degree of pleasure, different as they are, it must be that I find in myself the source of the effect which they produce.

The type of emotion peculiar to painting is, so to speak, *tangible;* poetry and music cannot give it. You enjoy the actual representation of objects as if you really saw them, and at the same time the meaning which the images have for the mind warms you and transports you. These figures, these objects, which seem the thing itself to a certain part of your intelligent being are like a solid bridge on which imagination supports itself to penetrate to the mysterious and profound sensation for which the forms are, so to speak, the hieroglyph, but a hieroglyph far more eloquent than a cold representation.

Eugène Delacroix
Journal (Oct. 20, 1853)

The scene represents Christopher Columbus and his son Diego upon their arrival at the Monastery of La Rábida, near the port of Palos. Delacroix's interpretation of the story follows the one made current by Washington Irving's *History of the Life and Voyages of Christopher Columbus,* which was published in both English and French in 1828. The architectural setting was suggested by the interior of the Carthusian monastery in Seville, sketched by Delacroix during his trip through Spain in 1832. Both this painting and its pendant, The Return of Columbus, in the Toledo (Ohio) Museum of Art, were painted for Prince Anatole Demidov. They were etched by Bracquemond. Collections: Prince Anatole Demidov, San Donato (near Florence); Édouard André, Paris; E. Secrétan, Paris; P. A. B. Widener, Philadelphia; Ferdinand Blumenthal; Count Cecil Pecci-Blunt, Rome. *Chester Dale Collection,* 1941. Canvas. Height 35⅝ in.; width 46⅜ in. (0.905 x 1.185). Signed, and dated 1838.

JEAN-BAPTISTE-CAMILLE COROT · French 1796-1875

Forest of Fontainebleau

"After my outings," Corot says, "I invite Nature to spend a few days with me; then begins my madness. Brush in hand, I hunt hazelnuts in the forests of my studio. I hear birds singing there, trees shivering in the wind. I see flowing brooks and rivers, laden with a thousand reflections of the sky and of all that lives on their banks. The sun rises and sets in my rooms". . . .

The most rapid sketch suffices him for a picture. I know of a very beautiful one, made in just one quarter of an hour at Fontainebleau. The sun is sinking behind the trees. A stream of light extends from the forest to the horizon, and contrasts strongly with the mass of foliage. "I will make a painting from this study," Corot said to me, "but, if it were necessary, I could now get along without having the sketch in front of me. When a collector wants a replica of one of my landscapes, I can easily give it to him without looking at the original again. I keep a copy of each of my works in my heart and in my eyes."

THÉOPHILE SILVESTRE
Histoire des artistes vivants (1857)

This is probably to be identified with the view of Fontainebleau that won favorable comments from the critics at the Salon of 1831. P. Burty, writing of the picture when it was exhibited at the École des Beaux-Arts in the year of the artist's death, says that Corot always considered this one of his best paintings and would have liked to buy it back, when it was owned by Binant, in order to offer it to the Louvre. It remained in Binant's collection from about 1855 until 1904. Collections: A. Binant, Paris; Crosdi, Paris. *Chester Dale Collection*, 1941. Canvas. Height 69 in.; width 95½ in. (1.75 x 2.43). Painted c. 1830.

EDOUARD MANET · French 1832-1883

The Dead Toreador

In all Manet's work there are not even two paintings which were not inspired by another painting, old or modern. Resolutely Manet took a composition from some canvas by a master, translated it into his own idiom, and began afresh the chosen work. The Spaniards, who influenced him so greatly, he imitated in his most beautiful manner, wishing to make museum pictures. No one plagiarized more than he, and no one is more original. Later, influenced by Claude Monet, he was to paint "plein-air" pictures, as many-colored as his first works were black and white, especially black. But always and everywhere the *touch* is Manet's own. His application of paint is unique; the awkwardness and at the same time the precision of his brush stroke, its decisiveness, belong only to him. . . .

It is because of his method that the work of Manet will live and compel recognition. Manet should have influenced his contemporaries by his excellent craftsmanship, but there was never any mention of his technical mastery until we discovered it, much later.

So we see that the same thing is repeated in the case of every painter. That which brings him to the attention of the experts, during his lifetime, is always the least interesting of his qualities. Some men benefit by the hour in which they make their appearance, from a fortuitous circumstance in their lifetime. Why has the name of Manet become a sort of reference point for the impressionists and the neo-impressionists? No one in modern art is related to him. Claude Monet mixed a new palette, Manet did not. The latter had no mannerisms, but there was a great deal of chance and variety in his inspiration. He was no theorist. His usual comments about his art were amiable and childish; he spoke of it as an amateur "communard" might speak of the revolution. His work is an exception, a sophistication, a curiosity. He added something piquant to everything he touched, something zestful, an unexpected charm. His work is a thing of chance — it is as decisive and unreasoned as that of a Ricard or a Gustave Moreau, we might even say of a Degas. These artists might have belonged to another place, another time. They are meteors in a night, in which thousands of wielders of brushes are indistinguishable. Manet excels inevitably by reason of his singular gift!

J.-É. Blanche
Essais et portraits (1912)

Manet seems to have appropriated in The Dead Toreador a composition he probably knew in a canvas entitled The Dead Warrior, attributed to the Spanish School of the seventeenth century, and now in the National Gallery in London. The two paintings are similar in shape and size, and have as their subject a single foreshortened figure of a dead man in much the same position. Manet may have seen The Dead Warrior when it was exhibited in the Louvre, or he may have known the engraving after it. In the Salon of 1864 he showed a large canvas entitled Épisode d'un Combat de Taureaux, with a dead toreador lying in the foreground. The critics complained that the composition lacked unity, and Manet accepted their judgment. He cut up the painting and preserved from it as a complete picture The Dead Toreador. Another fragment from his Salon painting is the Bull-Fight in the Frick Collection, New York. The present painting was etched by Manet in collaboration with Bracquemond in 1874. Collections: Jean-Baptiste Faure. *Widener Collection*, 1942. Canvas. Height 29¾ in.; width 60½ in. (0.755 x 1.536). Painted probably 1864, the year in which it was first exhibited.

EDGAR DEGAS · French 1834-1917

Madame René de Gas

Going through Paris for the review copies of *La Porte étroite,* I stop at the Valérys' to get news of Jeannie Valéry, on whom there was some question of operating. Degas is with her and has been wearing her out for more than an hour, for he is very hard of hearing and she has a weak voice. I find Degas has aged but is just like himself; just a bit more obstinate, more set in his opinion, exaggerating his crustiness, and always scratching the same spot in his brain where the itching becomes more and more localized. He says: "Ah, those who work from nature! What impudent humbugs! The landscapists! When I meet one of them in the countryside, I want to fire away at him. Bang! Bang!" (He raises his cane, closes an eye, and aims at the drawing-room furniture.) "There ought to be a police force for that purpose." Etc., etc. And again: "Art criticism! What an absurdity! I am accustomed to saying" (and in fact I remember hearing him say exactly the same things three or four years ago) "that the Muses never talk among themselves; each one works in her domain; and when they aren't working, they dance." And twice more he repeats: "When they aren't working, they dance." And again:

"The day when people began to write *Intelligence* with a capital *I,* all was damn well lost. There is no such thing as Intelligence; one has intelligence of this or that. One must have intelligence only for what one is doing."

André Gide
Journal (July 4, 1909)

In his correspondence Degas said of the subject of this portrait: "My poor Estelle, René's wife, is blind as you know. She bears it in an incomparable manner; she needs scarcely any help about the house. She remembers the rooms and the position of the furniture and hardly ever bumps into anything. And there is no hope! . . . She has borne him two children, she is going to give him a third whose Godfather I shall be, and as the widow of a young American killed in the war of Secession she already had a little girl of her own who is 9 years old. . . . The women here are almost all pretty and many have even amidst their charms that touch of ugliness without which, no salvation. But I fear that their heads are as weak as mine, which *à deux* would prove a strange guarantee for a new home. Alas, I have just let out something which is nothing and yet could earn me an atrocious reputation. . . . This is serious. There is no joking here. My death would not wipe out such an insult and Louisiana must be respected by all her children and I am almost one of them." Collections: Degas Sale, 1918; Henry D. Hughes, New York. *Chester Dale Collection,* 1941. Canvas. Height 28⅝ in.; width 36¼ in. (0.727 x 0.92). Painted in the winter of 1872-73, while the artist was visiting members of his family established in the cotton business in New Orleans.

MARY CASSATT · American 1845-1926

The Morning Toilet

I am suggesting that it [Impressionism] led directly to the rediscovery of paganism. The impressionist painters had to extract all the beauty and significance they required from their surroundings: they could depend neither on the intellectual additions and transformations nor on the traditional technical enrichments of the studio; nor were they permitted to eke out an artistic living by drawing on the dignity or picturesqueness of their theme. History and exoticism were taboo. In contemporary life they had to find all that they required, and contemporary life was lavish beyond their needs; so naturally they fell in love with it, and made the most exquisitely civilized of their generation and ours share their emotion.

When I say that the Impressionists fell in love with their surroundings I use the expression advisedly. At their best they are as lyrical as Fra Angelico himself:

> 'The world is so full of such wonderful things,
> I am sure we should all be as happy as kings.'

And you must remember that the wonderful things of which the world was so full had for years been considered inappropriate, if not inimical, to art.

CLIVE BELL
Landmarks in Nineteenth-Century Painting (1927)

They tell a story that one day, in front of Degas, Miss Cassatt, judging a well-known painter who was one of their friends, dared to say: "He has no style." Degas laughed, and shrugged his shoulders with a movement which signified: Look at these women who meddle with critical opinions! Do they even know what style is?

Miss Cassatt was annoyed. She chose for a model a very ugly woman, a servant of a coarse type. She had her pose in a chemise beside her toilet table with the gestures of a woman who is preparing for bed, her left hand grasping the thin tress of lifted hair at the neck, and the other drawing the tress to knot it. This girl is seen almost entirely in profile; her mouth hangs open; her expression is stupid and weary.

When Degas saw the picture, he wrote Miss Cassatt: "What design! What style!"

ACHILLE SEGARD
Mary Cassatt (1913)

The best nineteenth-century painters sought to use the tradition of the Old Masters to "extract all the beauty and significance they required from their surroundings." Mary Cassatt, for instance, has taken a famous Renaissance pose, the uplifted bent arm of the Bound Slave by Michelangelo now in the Louvre, to show the accidental beauty in the gesture of a young girl arranging her hair. So successful was Miss Cassatt's translation of the poetry of the Renaissance into the prose of the nineteenth century that her close friend Degas purchased the painting for his own collection, and it was sold only after his death. Collections: Edgar Degas, Paris; H. O. Havemeyer, New York. *Chester Dale Collection,* 1942. Canvas. Height 29½ in.; width 24⅝ in. (0.75 x 0.625). Painted 1886.

BERTHE MORISOT · French 1841-1895

The Mother and Sister of the Artist

To make poetry in the plastic arts demands that the artist portray on a surface the luminous secret of things, simply, directly, without extraneous detail; it requires the creation of a rich analysis of life, purely to restore it with alchemy — mobility and illusion. No intruding illumination of dreams, but on the other hand the banal is suppressed.

One may well take pleasure in the glow of children, the bloom of fruit, the flowering of adolescence, but with this tenderly it is finished. Our painter moves through her counterpart, a gala creature arranged in exotic gowns, elegant and minutely finished; revealing much less than the genre infers, the calligrapher, literally the novelist. By what clairvoyance, miracle, is the satin animated by its contact with the skin, the pearls given lustre in the atmosphere? Or by what means a perfect negligee in dress accomplished so that the absolute mundanity of style bursts forth in harmony with garden and beach? A classic mind clothes such fluidities with silver.

Fairyland, yes and the tangible world are intermingled by inspiration. Morning and afternoon are telescoped, like the gliding rush of swans alighting on water or the inordinate hurry of youth through the beautiful length of a day.

Stéphane Mallarmé
Berthe Morisot: Exposition de son œuvre (1896)

This double portrait was painted at Passy, where Mme. Pontillon (née Edma Morisot), the younger of the two sitters in the painting, had come to await the birth of her first child in the home of her parents. Correspondence between Berthe Morisot, Mme. Pontillon and their mother tells of the finishing of the picture (Rouart, 1950). Manet, according to the letters, had come to inspect the painting a few hours before it was sent for exhibition at the Salon of 1870. He seized the brush and spent the afternoon retouching the dress and face of Mme. Morisot's portrait. Berthe Morisot, we also know from the letters, felt at first that Manet had greatly marred the painting, but was reassured when she heard it praised by Fantin-Latour and others at the exhibition. Collections: Pontillon family, Paris. *Chester Dale Collection*, 1941. Canvas. Height 39¾ in.; width 32¼ in. (1.01 x 0.82). Painted during the winter of 1869-70.

CLAUDE MONET · FRENCH 1840-1926

Venice, Palazzo da Mula

With the death of Monet—less than twenty years ago—there disappeared the last master of that unique and astonishing pleiad which had constituted the impressionist group. He died, like Ingres, at a time when the ideas which he personified had long ceased to belong to actuality. The first of the impressionist painters to achieve success, the only one of them to see it turn into a real triumph, he lived to witness his isolation and must have felt some bitterness that the vision which it had taken so many years to impose was most violently attacked by the younger generations. Yet it was not the new art movements which preoccupied him during his last years but the past with which history will forever identify his name. In a letter written shortly before his death, he tried to sum up his contribution: "I have always had a horror of theories, . . . I have only the merit of having painted directly from nature, trying to convey my impressions in the presence of the most fugitive effects, and I am distressed at having been the cause of the name given to a group of which the majority was not at all impressionist."

This regret expressed by Monet in the evening of his life seems strange. Might he not have felt some pride in having provided, though involuntarily, a name for a movement that had added one of the most glorious chapters to the history of art? Forty years had passed since the group of Monet's friends had definitely dissolved, but impressionism was not dead because the men who had promoted it had ceased to be impressionists. Even though it was no longer a battle-cry, it remained a living inspiration to those who came afterwards. Its achievements had become the common heritage of mankind on which to base new conquests. It was true, though, that the younger generation had ended by discarding most of the impressionist principles, that fauvists, cubists, expressionists, futurists, dadaists, surrealists had opened entirely new horizons. But their efforts had been fertilized by Cézanne, Gauguin, van Gogh and Seurat, all of whom had gone through impressionist experiences. While the direct influence of impressionism on contemporary art may sometimes seem negligible, while of the great living masters only Bonnard has continued to develop a style of his own in a truly impressionist spirit, it was the art of Monet and his companions which broke down countless prejudices and opened the road for steadily increasing boldness of technique, of color and abstraction.

JOHN REWALD
The History of Impressionism (1946)

When Monet painted this view he was living in the Palazzo Barbaro, diagonally across the canal from the Palazzo da Mula and he was so entranced with the light effects of Venice that he wrote: "All this unusual light! It is so beautiful! I am spending wonderful moments here and can almost forget I am as old as I am." Collections: Arthur B. Emmons, Newport, Rhode Island; Henry D. Hughes, New York. *Chester Dale Collection,* 1942. Canvas. Height 24½ in.; width 32 in. (0.622 x 0.813). Signed, and dated 1908, the year of the artist's brief winter sojourn of less than two months in Venice.

CAMILLE PISSARRO · French 1830-1903

Peasant Woman

Remember that I have the temperament of a peasant, I am melancholy, harsh and savage in my works, it is only in the long run that I can expect to please, and then only those who have a grain of indulgence; but the eye of the passerby is too hasty and sees only the surface. Whoever is in a hurry will not stop for me. . . .

Sometimes I am horribly afraid to turn round canvases which I have piled against the wall; I am constantly afraid of finding monsters where I believed there were precious gems! . . . However, at times I come across works of mine which are soundly done and really in my style, and at such moments I find great solace. But no more of that. Painting, art in general, enchants me. It is my life. What else matters? When you put all your soul into a work, all that is noble in you, you cannot fail to find a kindred soul who understands you, and you do not need a host of such spirits. Is not that all an artist should wish for? . . .

I do not believe that anyone could devote — if not more talent — more care and good will to the service of his art; it takes me hours of reflection to decide on the slightest detail; is this impatience? . . . I think not! For I do not wish to make a brush stroke when I do not feel complete mastery of my subject, there's the rub — that is the great difficulty; without sensation, nothing, absolutely nothing valid. . . .

One can make such beautiful things with so little. The motifs that are too beautiful sometimes appear even theatrical — just look at Switzerland. Old Corot, didn't he make beautiful little paintings in Gisors, two willows, a little stream, a bridge, like the painting at the Universal Exhibition? What a masterpiece! Happy are those who see beauty in the modest spots where others see nothing. Everything is beautiful, the whole secret lies in knowing how to interpret.

CAMILLE PISSARRO
Letters to His Son Lucien (1883-1893)

The painting reproduced is one of Pissarro's rare figure studies and is more significant than appears at first glance. For it is a challenge to the basic theory of Impressionism. In the search for momentary effects of light, the Impressionist painters had tended to neglect mass and volume. Substance for them often became merely an abstraction of light, a surface on which light revealed itself in certain patterns. In the Peasant Woman, however, Pissarro used the Impressionist technique of strokes of pure color to suggest the solid volumes of the figure. Though his aim was the traditional goal of Renaissance art, he was right in thinking "only in the long run. . . . I can expect to please," for the Peasant Woman was not sold in his lifetime and passed directly from the possession of his widow to the Chester Dale Collection. Collections: the widow of the artist. *Chester Dale Collection*, 1942. Canvas. Height 28¾ in.; width 23⅝ in. (0.73 x 0.60). Signed, and dated 1880.

AUGUSTE RENOIR · French 1841-1919

The Dancer

"You would say that he should work his problem out by study of nature, would you not?" Renoir hesitates a moment over the great word: Monet and Cézanne, among his old comrades, had always talked of nature, and the word had a sort of halo around it, anyhow. But finally he determines to speak out:

"No; nature brings men to isolation. I want to stay in the ranks."

"But the schools being bad, as you have said, if it is not before nature, where is it that the young man becomes an artist?"

"Au musée, parbleu!"

It was at the Museum that he himself had served his apprenticeship in the time-honored procedure of copying the masters, as Ingres, a few days before his death at the age of eighty-seven, was still doing; as Delacroix had done, with his profoundly analytical mind; as the rough mountaineer Courbet did with his grandly heavy brush; as Manet did with the eclecticism of his old culture; as Degas did with his severely classical intelligence; as Redon did in order to situate his world of vision within the sphere of reality which he saw in the great draftsmen; as Seurat did to strengthen the scientific basis of his painting with the greater authority of art. All these men were the "moderns" of their respective periods, and what is more, all of them could make their intense use of the classics and yet retain their originality intact. Of course, no one would accuse Renoir of being unaware of the fact that artists of the greatest merit have studied at schools or under teachers or from nature. What he meant, as is quite clear, was that the deciding factor in the formation of an art is, after all, the influence — direct or indirect — of the classics we have heard him discuss before. The Museum has been the real teacher of all great men — of the present and the past, even if it is powerless against the incapacity of little men.

Walter Pach
Ananias or the False Artist (1928)

As a pupil, Fougères had studied design under Servin, who passed in the academic world as a great draftsman. Later, he had worked under Schinner, in order to discover the secrets of the powerful and magnificent color which distinguishes that master. But the master, and his disciples, had been cautious; Fougères found out nothing. From there, Fougères had passed to the studio of Sommervieux in order to familiarize himself with that aspect of art called Composition; but Composition was shy and escaped him. He had next tried to wrest from Granet and Drolling the mystery of their interior effects; but the two masters had not permitted themselves to be robbed. Finally, Fougères had finished his training with Duval-Lecamus.

Honoré de Balzac
Pierre Grassou (1840)

As Balzac shows through the life of his imaginary painter Fougères, in the art schools of the nineteenth century the student was not taught in the collaborative fashion of the Old Masters as described by Samuel Butler on page 54. Hence the best students gradually abandoned the schools and learned to paint in the museums. Collections: Deudon, Paris. *Widener Collection*, 1942. Canvas. Height 56⅛ in.; width 37⅛ in. (1.425 x 0.945). Signed, and dated 1874.

PAUL CEZANNE · French 1839-1906

Vase of Flowers

Alanson Hartpence was employed at the Daniel Gallery. One day, the proprietor being out, Hartpence was in charge. In walked one of their most important customers, a woman in her fifties who was much interested in some picture whose identity I may at one time have known. She liked it, and seemed about to make the purchase, walked away from it, approached it and said, finally, "But Mr. Hartpence, what is all that down in this left hand lower corner?"

Hartpence came up close and carefully inspected the area mentioned. Then, after further consideration, "That, Madam," said he, "is paint."

This story marks the exact point in the transition that took place, in the world of that time, from the appreciation of a work of art as a copying of nature to the thought of it as the imitation of nature, spoken of by Aristotle in his *Poetics,* which has since governed our conceptions. It is still the failure to take this step that blocks us in seeking to gain a full conception of the modern in art.

In painting Cézanne is the first consciously to have taken that step. From him it went on, often by nothing more than the *vis a tergo,* rushing through the gap where the dyke has been broken. But with such a man as Braque it had basic significance. Braque is said to have taken his pictures outdoors, on occasion, to see if their invention ranked beside that of nature worthily enough for him to approve of it.

Almost no one seems to realize that this movement is straight from the *Poetics,* misinterpreted for over two thousand years and more. The objective is not to copy nature and never was, but to imitate nature, which involved active invention, the active work of the imagination invoked by such a person as Virginia Woolf. A man makes a picture, it is made of paint upon canvas stretched on a frame. In spite of endless talk, this has never been sufficiently brought out.

William Carlos Williams
The Autobiography of William Carlos Williams (1951)

I have not reproduced Nature, I have represented it. How? By its plastic and colored equivalents.

Paul Cézanne

The elaborate Baroque vase, almost as if bursting from the explosive force of the flowers, suggests a germinating seed pod. Thus Cézanne conveys symbolically the dynamic power of fertility. Yet, because he worked so slowly that flowers wilted before he could paint them, he used as a model for his picture the engraving of some other artist. Here is evidence that to imitate nature in the Aristotelian sense it is not necessary to paint from nature. Collections: Gustave Caillebotte, Paris. *Chester Dale Collection,* 1942. Canvas. Height 28¾ in.; width 23⅜ in. (0.73 x 0.60). Painted c. 1875.

PAUL GAUGUIN · French 1848-1903

Fatata te Miti

In the visual arts, indeed, 'the fall of man into his own circumference' seems at an end, and when I look at the photograph of a picture by Gauguin, which hangs over my breakfast table, the spectacle of tranquil Polynesian girls crowned with lilies gives me, I do not know why, religious ideas. Our appreciations of the older schools are changing too, becoming simpler, and when we take pleasure in some Chinese painting of an old man, meditating upon a mountain path, we share his meditation, without forgetting the beautiful intricate pattern of the lines like those we have seen under our eye-lids as we fell asleep; nor do the Bride and Bridegroom of Rajput painting, sleeping upon a house-top, or wakening when out of the still water the swans fly upward at the dawn, seem the less well painted because they remind us of many poems. We are becoming interested in expression in its first phase of energy, when all the arts play like children about the one chimney and turbulent innocence can yet amuse those brisk and active men who have paid us so little attention of recent years. Shall we be rid of the pride of intellect, of sedentary meditation, of emotion that leaves us when the book is closed or the picture seen no more; and live amid the thoughts that can go with us by steam-boat and railway as once upon horse-back, or camel-back, rediscovering, by our re-integration of the mind, our more profound Pre-Raphaelitism, the old abounding, nonchalant reverie?

WILLIAM BUTLER YEATS
Art and Ideas (1913)

A great artist is like a fig-tree whose roots run a hundred feet underground, in search of tea-leaves, cinders and old boots. Art which is directly produced for the Community can never have the same withdrawn quality as that which is made out of the artist's solitude. For this possesses the integrity and bleak exhilaration that are to be gained only from the absence of an audience and from communion with the primal sources of unconscious life. One cannot serve both beauty and power: "Le pouvoir est essentiellement stupide." A public figure can never be an artist, and no artist should ever become one unless his work is done, and he chooses to retire into public life.

An artist grows into a public figure through being always willing to address strangers. "Pauvre et sans honneurs," wrote Valéry of Mallarmé, "la nudité de sa condition avilissait tous les avantages des autres . . . Tout leur semblait naïf et lâche après qu'ils l'avaient lu."

CYRIL CONNOLLY
The Unquiet Grave (1945)

Yeats states the Romantic point of view that art is concerned with more than formal values. Its purpose is also to stimulate "the old abounding, nonchalant reverie." For Yeats the beauty of Gauguin's paintings consists in the ideas they evoke, the poems they suggest. Speaking of his work in the Marquesas, Gauguin asked: "Are not these repetitions of tone, these monotonous color harmonies (in the musical sense) analogous to oriental chants sung in a shrill voice to the accompaniment of pulsating notes which intensify them by contrast?" When he painted the picture reproduced, Gauguin was living among the natives. Tehoura, a Polynesian of great beauty, became his *vahine* and probably posed for the girl on the right removing her sarong. Collections: Ambroise Vollard, Paris; Louis Horch, New York. *Chester Dale Collection*, 1942. Canvas. Height 26¾ in.; width 36 in. (0.68 x 0.915). Signed, and dated 1892.

VINCENT VAN GOGH · Dutch 1853-1890

The Olive Orchard

I turned into a side street. There in a house was a respectable-looking store without a display window, and at the entrance a sign: Comprehensive Exhibition of Paintings and Drawings. I read the name of the artist, but at once forgot it. I had not entered a museum nor an art gallery for twenty years; but somehow, and this was the important thing at the moment, I thought it would divert my mind from its mad imagining. So I went in. . . .

There were about sixty paintings. . . . At first sight they seemed to me glaring and restless, altogether raw and strange. I had to grope my way before the first one registered as a picture at all, as a coherent thing. But then, then I saw them all thus, each one singly, and all of them together. I saw Nature in them and the human intelligence that had fashioned this Nature — the tree and bush and field and slope which were painted there. I perceived also something else, something behind the painted forms, an essence, an indescribable harmony. All this impressed me so strongly that in these pictures I lost my awareness of self; then regained it again powerfully; then lost it! . . .

How can I make it comprehensible to you that in these paintings each entity — every tree, every furrow of yellow or green field, every fence, the gorge cut through the stony hill, the pewter jug, the earthenware bowl, the table, the clumsy chair — rose up to me as if newborn from the grim chaos of inanimation, from the abyss of nonentity. I felt — No! I knew! — that each of those created things was born from a terrible uncertainty about the world, and had now, by the fact of its very existence, sealed over for all time some dread yawning chasm of nonexistence. How can I make it even half clear to you the way this language spoke to my soul, thrusting at me this tremendous justification of the strangest, most inexplicable state of my inner being. It made me comprehend at once what in my extreme depression I could scarcely endure, and what nevertheless — how strongly I sensed this! — I could no longer tear out of myself. In this place an unknown soul of incomprehensible power gave me the answer, answered me with a whole new world! I felt like one who, after endless stumbling, finds firm ground beneath his feet, and longs to shout exultantly into the tempest raging about him. . . .

P. S. The man is called Vincent van Gogh.

HUGO VON HOFMANNSTHAL
Letter to a friend (May 26, 1901)

This is one of three versions of the composition, all approximately equal in size, which Van Gogh discusses in letters written from Saint-Rémy in November, 1889. One of the versions, "a canvas worked at from memory after the study of the same size done on the spot," was intended for his mother and sister; "a repetition of it and the study" were for his brother, Theo. Collections: Dr. Fritz A. Moll, Brieg (near Breslau); Julius Stern, Berlin. *Chester Dale Collection*, 1942. Canvas. Height 28¾ in.; width 36¼ in. (0.73 x 0.92). Painted 1889.

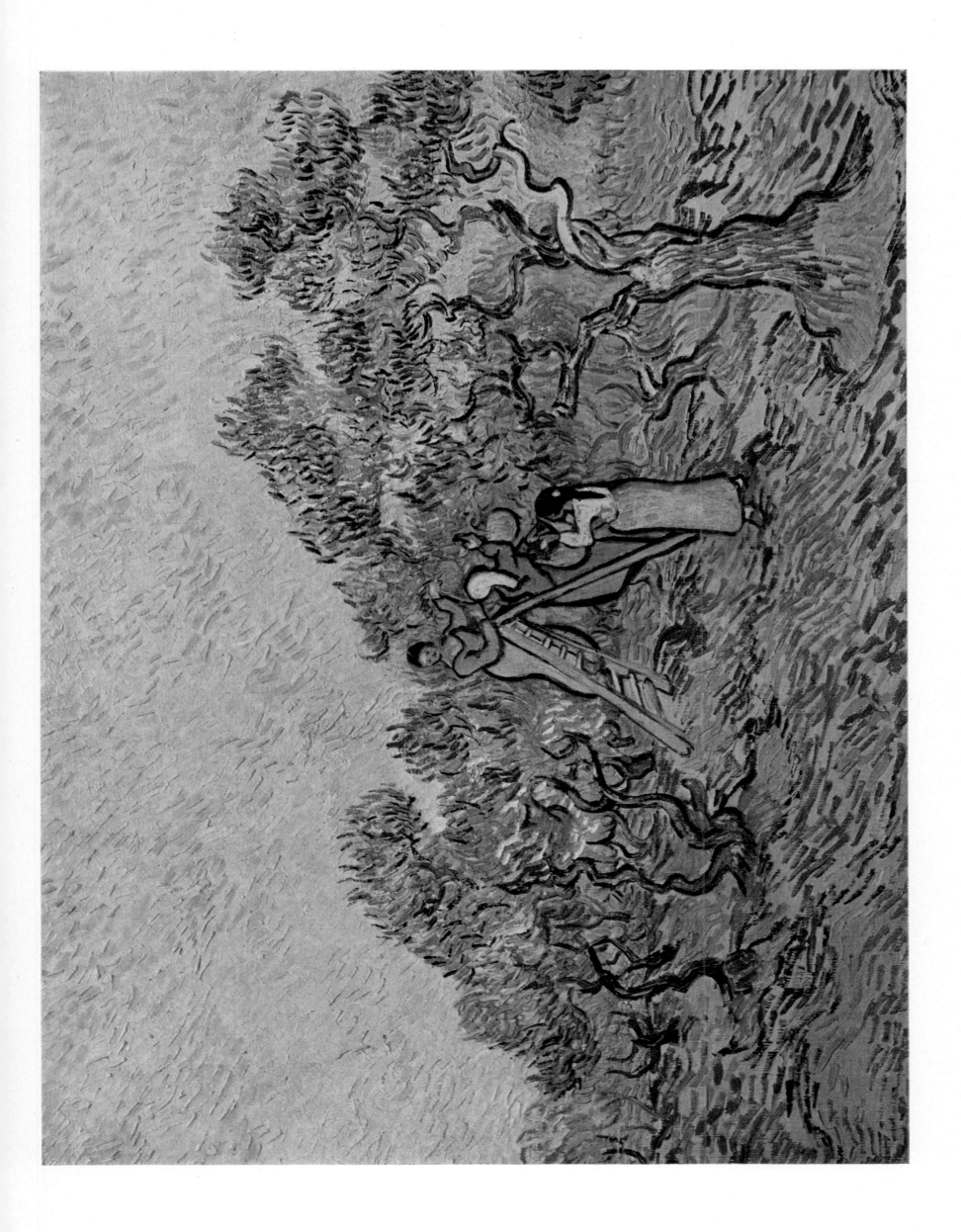

HENRI ROUSSEAU · French 1844-1910

The Equatorial Jungle

It is not the jungle as a botanical or zoological park that he paints, but the jungle of terror and beauty that we dreamed about as children, where palm-forests gleam in silver moonlight along broad rivers, where walls of trees stand, with gigantic blackish-green leaves, and large exotic birds sit motionless, where the lion lies in the high rushes, and monkeys chatter in the pale green treetops, where in the night one hears the scream of a native being killed by a panther, and the flute of a black woman who charms the snakes from their hiding places. This is not the jungle we see in motion pictures, but the jungle as an imaginative experience. They say that when Rousseau painted these pictures he was so stricken with the power of his own imagination that, overcome with fear and oppression, he had to open the window for air.

WILHELM UHDE
Henri Rousseau (1921)

Only after rigorous proof of his ability did he succeed in gaining the recognition of his fellow artists. He has become more and more perfect in the original genre he adopted, and is in a fair way to becoming one of our best realist painters.

He sports a bushy beard as a mark of distinction, and has for some time now been a member of the Independents, holding that complete freedom of action should be left to the creator whose mind aspires to the realm of the Good and the Beautiful.

HENRI ROUSSEAU
Autobiographical Note (July 10, 1895)

Critic and artist often disagree. Uhde's interpretation of Rousseau's work corresponds with the general impression his pictures convey. Yet Rousseau in his own words considers himself a realist; we know from his friends that he wished to render nature accurately and that he admired the technical skill of academic painters, such as Bouguereau and Courtois. The canvas reproduced was painted the year before the artist's death. It is thought such scenes may recall the jungle Rousseau had known as a young man when he is believed to have served in the army of the Emperor Maximilian in Mexico. If so, these impressions were later revivified by frequent observations and studies made in the botanical gardens and zoo in Paris. His third-person account of himself, quoted above, was written originally for a biographical dictionary of artists. Collections: Robert Delaunay, Paris. *Chester Dale Collection*, 1942. Canvas. Height 55¼ in.; width 51 in. (1.403 x 1.295). Signed, and dated 1909.

GEORGE INNESS · AMERICAN 1825-1894

The Lackawanna Valley

Editor Ledger:

A copy of your letter has been handed to me in which I find your art editor has classified my work among the "Impressionists." The article is certainly all that I could ask in the way of compliment. I am sorry, however, that either of my works should have been so lacking in the necessary detail that from a legitimate landscape-painter I have come to be classed as a follower of the new fad "Impressionism". . . .

We are all the subjects of impressions, and some of us legitimates seek to convey our impressions to others. In the art of communicating impressions lies the power of generalizing without losing that logical connection of parts to the whole which satisfies the mind.

The elements of this, therefore, are solidity of objects and transparency of shadows in a breathable atmosphere through which we are conscious of spaces and distances. By the rendering of these elements we suggest the invisible side of visible objects. These elements constitute the grammar of painting, and the want of that grammar gives to pictures either the flatness of the silhouette or the vulgarity of an over-strained objectivity or the puddling twaddle of Preraphaelism. . . .

When people tell me that the painter sees nature in the way the Impressionists paint it, I say, "Humbug!" from the lie of intent to the lie of ignorance.

Monet induces the humbug of the first form and the stupidity of the second. Through malformed eyes we see imperfectly and are subjects for the optician. Though the normally formed eye sees within degrees of distinctness and without blur we want for good art sound eyesight. It is well known that we through the eye realize the objective only through the experiences of life. All is flat, and the mind is in no realization of space except its powers are exercised through the sense of feeling. That is, what is objective to us is a response to the universal principle of truth.

GEORGE INNESS
Letter (1884)

George Inness, Jr., son of the painter, describes in *Life, Art and Letters of George Inness,* 1917, how his father went to Scranton as a young man "for the purpose of making a painting of the first roundhouse on the D.L.&W. Railroad, which was to be used for advertising. There was in reality only one track at the time running into the roundhouse, but the president of the road insisted on having four or five painted in, easing his conscience by explaining that the road would eventually have them. Pop protested, but the president was adamant, and there was a family to support, so the tracks were painted in. In the busy years which followed, the picture was virtually forgotten until thirty years or more afterward, when my mother and father were in the City of Mexico, they discovered the old canvas in a junk-shop. The shopkeeper knew nothing of its origin or who painted it, and explained that he had bought it with a job lot of office furnishings, and would be glad to sell it cheap. So my father purchased it for old time's sake. As he walked out of the shop he said, 'Do you remember, Lizzie, how mad I was because they made me paint the name on the engine?' " The crudely written letter by Inness himself which is quoted in part at the top of this page reflects the attitude toward Impressionism of those American painters who derived their style from the Barbizon School. Collections: Delaware, Lackawanna & Western Railroad; Mrs. Jonathan Scott Hartley, the artist's daughter, New York. *Gift of Mrs. Huttleston Rogers,* 1945. Canvas. Height 33⅞ in.; width 50¼ in. (0.86 x 1.275). Painted 1855.

WINSLOW HOMER · American 1836-1910

Right and Left

He had bought a pair of wild ducks for Thanksgiving. Their plumage was so handsome that he was tempted to paint them, and before he was through, his Thanksgiving dinner was spoiled. They were shown having just taken wing from the waves and being brought down by two shots from a double-barrelled shotgun. As usual he studied the subject thoroughly, going out day after day with a hunter in a boat and observing the birds' actions when they were shot. He even posted himself on the shore and got the man to shoot towards him, to see what the flash looked like; but he admitted that he never did, for he closed his eyes each time. An odd conception, with all his characteristic ability to create art out of unlikely subjects, the picture is at once engagingly naïve and a brilliant tour de force. The ducks' striking black, white and gray plumage against green waves and gray and pale gold sky, has a decorative beauty that reminds one of Audubon.

Lloyd Goodrich
Winslow Homer (1944)

He had no title for the picture. It was sent to Knoedler & Company's gallery in New York; a sportsman came in, caught a glimpse of the picture, and at once cried out: "Right and left!"— admiring, not so much the picture *per se*, as the skill of the hunter who could bring down a bird with each barrel of his double-barreled shotgun in quick succession. So the work was christened.

William Howe Downes
The Life and Works of Winslow Homer (1911)

This was the next to last canvas executed by Winslow Homer. It shows not only his painstaking realism but also a mastery of pattern, which at the end of his life marked a new development in his style. As in many other painters, Cosimo Tura or Pater for example (see pages 43 and 121), there is a repetition of shapes. The jagged edge of the white wave is echoed in the silhouette of the falling ducks, to give a decorative rhythm to the design. The asymmetry of the composition, however, suggests the influence of Japanese prints rather than of Renaissance or Rococo painting. Collections: Randal Morgan, Chestnut Hill, Philadelphia. *Given by the Avalon Foundation through the generosity of Ailsa Mellon Bruce,* 1951. Canvas. Height 28¼ in.; width 48½ in. (0.718 x 1.23). Signed, and dated 1909.

ALBERT PINKHAM RYDER · American 1847-1917

Siegfried and the Rhine Maidens

Ryder has for once transcribed all outer semblances by means of a personality unrelated to anything other than itself, an imagination belonging strictly to our soil and specifically to our Eastern geography. In his autographic quality he is certainly our finest genius, the most creative, the most racial. For our genius, at its best, is the genius of the evasive; we are born lovers of the secret element, the mystery in things.

How many of our American painters have given real attention to Ryder? I find him so much the legend among professional artists, this master of arabesque, this first and foremost of our designers, this real creator of pattern, this first of all creators of tragic landscape, whose pictures are sacred to those that revere distinction and power in art. He had in him that finer kind of reverence for the element of beauty which finds all things somehow lovely. He understood best of all the meaning of the grandiose, of everything that is powerful; none of his associates in point of time rose to just that sublimated experience; not Fuller, not Martin, not Blakelock, though each of these was touched to a special expression. They are more derivative than Ryder, more the children of Barbizon.

Ryder gave us first and last an incomparable sense of pattern and austerity of mood. He saw with an all too pitiless and pitiful eye the element of helplessness in things, the complete succumbing of things in nature to those elements greater than they that wield a fatal power. Ryder was the last of the romantics, the last of that great school of impressive artistry, as he was the first of our real painters and the greatest in vision. He was a still companion of Blake in that realm of the beyond, the first citizen of the land of Luthany. He knew the fine distinction between drama and tragedy, the tragedy which nature prevails upon the sensitive to accept. He was the painter poet of the immanent in things.

Marsden Hartley
Adventures in the Arts (1921)

The scene of the painting is from Act III of Wagner's Götterdämmerung. Daingerfield (*Scribner's Magazine*, March, 1918) quotes Ryder as saying to him: "I had been to hear the opera and went home about 12 o'clock and began this picture. I worked for 48 hours without sleep or food, and the picture was the result." Ryder sold the painting to the Montreal collector Sir William Van Horne, whom he often visited. Collections: Sir William Cornelius Van Horne, Montreal. *Mellon Collection*, 1946. Canvas. Height 19⅞ in.; width 20½ in. (0.505 x 0.52). Painted between 1875 and 1891, when it was first exhibited in New York.

GEORGE BELLOWS · AMERICAN 1882-1925

Both Members of This Club

It is the struggle alone that gives us pleasure, not the victory. We like to see animals fighting, not the victor worrying the vanquished — it is the gaining of the victory that we enjoy; but, immediately that is won, we are surfeited. As in a game of skill, so it is in the search for truth. In disputes we like the clash of opinion, but not at all to contemplate truth when it is found. To observe truth with pleasure, it must be seen emerging from strife. It is the same with the passions — there is pleasure in perceiving the collision of two contraries; but as soon as one gains the mastery, the conflict becomes mere brutality.

We never pursue things for themselves, but only for the pursuit. So it is in the theatre — scenes of happiness, not countered by apprehension, are worthless, as are episodes of extreme misery, brutal love or ruthless punishment, when hope is withheld.

BLAISE PASCAL
Pensées (1670)

A work of art is both independent of and dependent on a subject; independent in that all objective or subjective sensations, anything, in fact, which has the power to hold or receive human attention, may be the subject of a work of art; dependent, in the sense of the necessity, whether realised or not, of a point of departure, a kernel, a unit established, around which the creative imagination builds or weaves itself. The name given to a thing is *not* the subject, it is only a convenient label. Any subject is inexhaustible.

GEORGE BELLOWS
The Paintings of George Bellows (1929)

Athletic contests, especially boxing, inspired many of Bellows' best paintings. He looked on Sharkey's athletic club, where the present scene took place, as the most exciting of art classes. Until 1920 in New York fights were legal only if held in a club and participated in by club members. Hence the title of the picture. It has proved impossible to identify the fighters, though it has been suggested that they were Joe Gans and Kid Russell. Assuming the correctness of Pascal's generalization, Bellows has seized the moment in the contest to give the spectator optimum pleasure. Collections: Mrs. George Bellows, New York. *Gift of Chester Dale*, 1945. Canvas. Height 45¼ in.; width 63⅛ in. (1.15 x 1.605). Painted 1909.

APPENDIX

ANONYMOUS, *Pervigilium Veneris* (see page 60)

Cras amet qui nunquam amavit quique amavit cras amet:
ver novum, ver iam canorum, ver renatus orbis est;
vere concordant amores, vere nubunt alites,
et nemus comam resolvit de maritis imbribus.

cras amet qui nunquam amavit quique amavit cras amet.

cras erit cum primus aether copulavit nuptias:
tunc cruore de superno spumeo et ponti globo,
caerulas inter catervas, inter et bipedes equos,
fecit undantem Dionem de maritis imbribus.

cras amet qui nunquam amavit quique amavit cras amet.

iussus est inermis ire, nudus ire iussus est,
neu quid arcu neu sagitta neu quid igne laederet:
sed tamen cavete nymphae, quod Cupido pulcher est:
totus est inermis idem quando nudus est Amor.

cras amet qui nunquam amavit quique amavit cras amet.

pervium sui tenorem seminali tramite
perque caelum perque terras perque pontum subditum
ipsa duxit, ipsa venis procreantem spiritum
inbuit, iussitque mundum nosse nascendi vias.

cras amet qui nunquam amavit quique amavit cras amet.

DANCOURT, *Les Festes nocturnes du cours* (see page 120)

To make fresh conquests, love lures all Paris to the Mall. Time and again in the moonlight the Belles change their Beaux, and are scarcely more faithful to their sweethearts than to their husbands.

Dissimulate, Demoiselles, the secret ardors that consume you under the sway of the god of love, conceal well the desire he inspires. But if martyrdom compels you to speak, let yourself be drawn to the festivities in the Mall.

You beauties who yearn for love, why defend yourselves against it? It is not easy to kindle love's fires without being burned.

VIRGIL, *Aeneid* (see page 80)

Hic aliud maius miseris multoque tremendum
obicitur magis atque improvida pectora turbat.
Laocoon, ductus Neptuno sorte sacerdos,
sollemnis taurum ingentem mactabat ad aras.
ecce autem gemini a Tenedo tranquilla per alta
(horresco referens) immensis orbibus angues
incumbunt pelago pariterque ad litora tendunt:
pectora quorum inter fluctus arrecta iubaeque
sanguineae superant undas; pars cetera pontum
pone legit sinuatque immensa volumine terga.
fit sonitus spumante salo; iamque arva tenebant
ardentisque oculos suffecti sanguine et igni
sibila lambebant linguis vibrantibus ora.
diffugimus visu exsangues. illi agmine certo
Laocoonta petunt; et primum parva duorum
corpora natorum serpens amplexus uterque
implicat et miseros morsu depascitur artus;
post ipsum, auxilio subeuntem ac tela ferentem
corripiunt spirisque ligant ingentibus: et iam
bis medium amplexi, bis collo squamea circum
terga dati, superant capite et cervicibus altis.
ille simul manibus tendit divellere nodos,
perfusus sanie vittas atroque veneno,
clamores simul horrendos ad sidera tollit,
qualis mugitus, fugit cum saucius aram
taurus et incertam excussit cervice securim.
at gemini lapsu delubra ad summa dracones
effugiunt saevaeque petunt Tritonidis arcem,
sub pedibusque deae clipeique sub orbe teguntur.

VIRGIL, *Georgics* (see page 114)

At vero Zephyris cum laeta vocantibus aestas
in saltus utrumque gregem atque in pascua mittet,
Luciferi primo cum sidere frigida rura
carpamus, dum mane novum, dum gramina canent,
et ros in tenera pecori gratissimus herba.
inde ubi quarta sitim caeli collegerit hora
et cantu querulae rumpent arbusta cicadae,
ad puteos aut alta greges ad stagna iubebo
currentem ilignis potare canalibus undam;
aestibus at mediis umbrosam exquirere vallem,
sicubi magna Iovis antiquo robore quercus
ingentis tendat ramos, aut sicubi nigrum
ilicibus crebris sacra nemus accubet umbra;
tum tenuis dare rursus aquas et pascere rursus
solis ad occasum, cum frigidus aëra vesper
temperat, et saltus reficit iam roscida luna
litoraque alcyonem resonant, acalanthida dumi.